ALFRED WALLIS SKETCHBOOKS

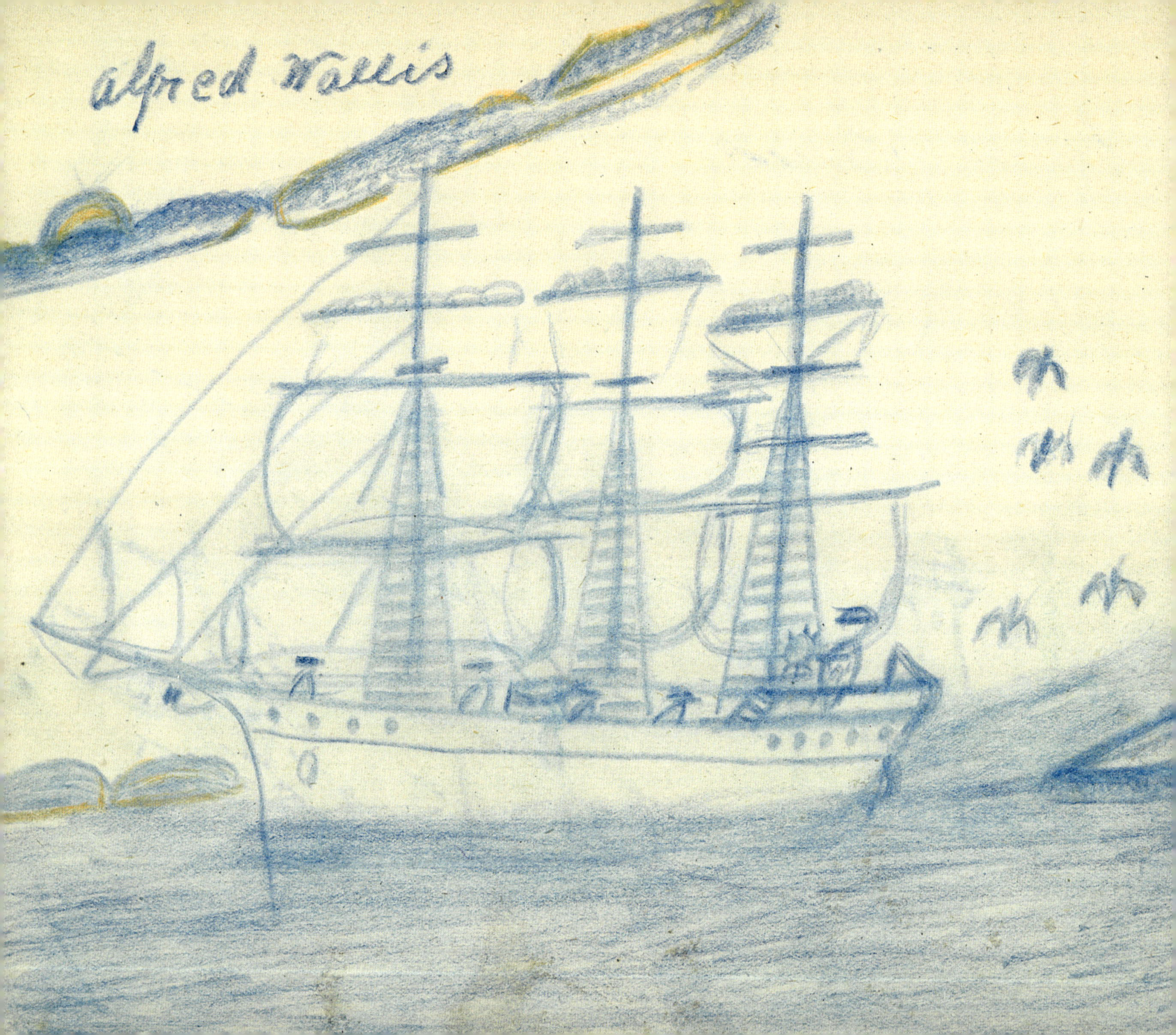

alfred wallis

ALFRED WALLIS
SKETCHBOOKS

With an introduction by
Andrew Wilson

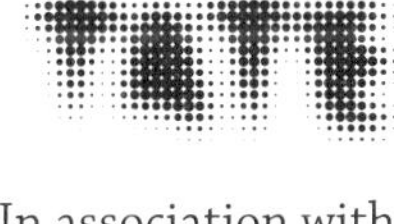

In association with
Kettle's Yard

First published 2023 by order of the Tate Trustees
by Tate Publishing, a division of Tate Enterprises Ltd,
Millbank, London SW1P 4RG
www.tate.org.uk/publishing

A catalogue record for this book is available from the
British Library

ISBN 978 1 84976 818 4

Distributed in the United States and Canada by
ABRAMS, New York

Library of Congress Control Number applied for

Project Editor: Nicola Bion
Production: Roanne Marner
Picture Research: Emma O'Neill
Designed by Susan Wightman, Libanus Press Ltd
Colour reproduction by DL Imaging Ltd, London
Printed and bound in China by C&C Offset Printing Co., Ltd

Cover: Alfred Wallis, *Grey Book* 1942 (details,
see pp.26–7)
Frontispiece: Alfred Wallis, *Lion Book* 1942 (detail,
see p.43)

Measurements of artworks are given in centimetres,
height before width
Grey Book: 23.5 × 30
Lion Book: 21.5 × 29
Castle Book: 21.5 × 28

The original orientation of the sketches has been
retained.

All works were purchased jointly by Tate and Kettle's
Yard with funds provided by the National Heritage
Memorial Fund, Tate Members, Friends of Kettle's Yard
and with Art Fund Support 2020 © Tate and Kettle's
Yard, with the exception of the following:
© Kettle's Yard, University of Cambridge pp.6, 8, 11, 12
© Tate, 2022 p.15

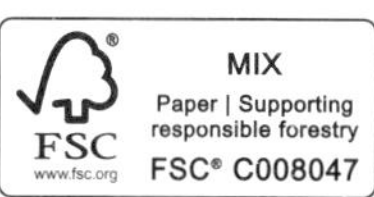

CONTENTS

Alfred Wallis: 'over the jasper sea'   7

Andrew Wilson

Grey Book   17

Lion Book   39

Castle Book   63

Ap 6 1935

Dear sir i Receved
your letter with Thanks
and also The pantins wich you
Did not want
what i do mosley is what
use To bee out of my own
memery what we may never
see again as Thing are altered
all To gether Ther is nothin
what Ever do not look like
what it was sence i can kember
if i live Till The 8 of august
next i shall be 78 years old
i was Born in Devenport
Born on The day of The fall
of Serveserpool Rushan war
so i cos from your
     friend alfred wallis

ALFRED WALLIS: 'OVER THE JASPER SEA'

St Ives projects an image that, for many people, is closely identified with the paintings of Alfred Wallis. Through his paintings Wallis brought his memories to life – memories of North Atlantic voyages among icebergs, of chasing the herring and mackerel seasons around the coast of Britain, and of inland landscapes. He created pictures that express a life of struggle and hardship as much as his religious belief. His paintings communicate directly, giving tangible and accurate evidence of that life. Yet they became directly aligned with, and had a profound effect on, the work of Ben and Winifred Nicholson and Christopher Wood in the late 1920s – and again for Ben Nicholson after he moved from London to St Ives in 1939. These artists were captivated more by their material and aesthetic response to his work – how Wallis's memories were painted and composed on these irregular pierces of torn and cut card, rather than what the painted memories might tell us about the experiences of Wallis's life. By the 1980s – forty years after his death – the extent to which St Ives was understood as a particular locus and crucible for modern art was signalled by Wallis's paintings. They described the place in a direct and unselfconscious way, and those qualities that had been sought out by Nicholson and others became a part of what ultimately defined St Ives as an 'art colony'. His paintings were celebrated as both modernist object and also as emotionally rooted to a particular place.

Amid such tensions, it is hard to connect with Alfred Wallis as a person rather than as a signifying cypher. Wallis was born in 1855 in Devonport, Plymouth. His parents Charles and Jane were originally from West Penwith and had married in 1844 in Penzance, moving to Devonport not long after. Charles was a labourer, working in a coach factory at the time of Alfred's birth (stories of him having enlisted to fight in the Crimean War and missing the birth seem to be apocryphal). Alfred's brother Charles was born two years earlier, while an elder daughter registered in 1851 has vanished from the records.[1] In 1866, after Alfred's mother died of tuberculosis, Charles moved with his two sons back to Penzance where he worked first as a paver and later as a basket weaver. It is clear that life would have been tough for the now motherless family (Charles did not remarry) and so it is hardly surprising that, as a child, Alfred may have started working. It also seems probable that he first went to sea at the age of nine, in a schooner across the Bay of Biscay.[2] In 1871 Alfred is registered as an 'apprentice basket maker' and his father as a 'journeyman mason'; in 1876 he is registered as both 'sailor' and a 'mariner, merchant service', but as a 'labourer' once again in 1879 and 1881.

It is in 1876 that there is documentary evidence to show that Wallis crossed the Atlantic as an 'ordinary seaman' on *The Pride of the West*, sailing from Penzance to Cadiz before continuing on to Newfoundland. At St John's he left that ship, joining another boat, the *Belle Aventure*, which arrived in Teignmouth in November 1876 after a gruelling three-month crossing. The challenging nature of the voyage and the fact that Wallis moved with relative ease from one ship to another for his return indicates

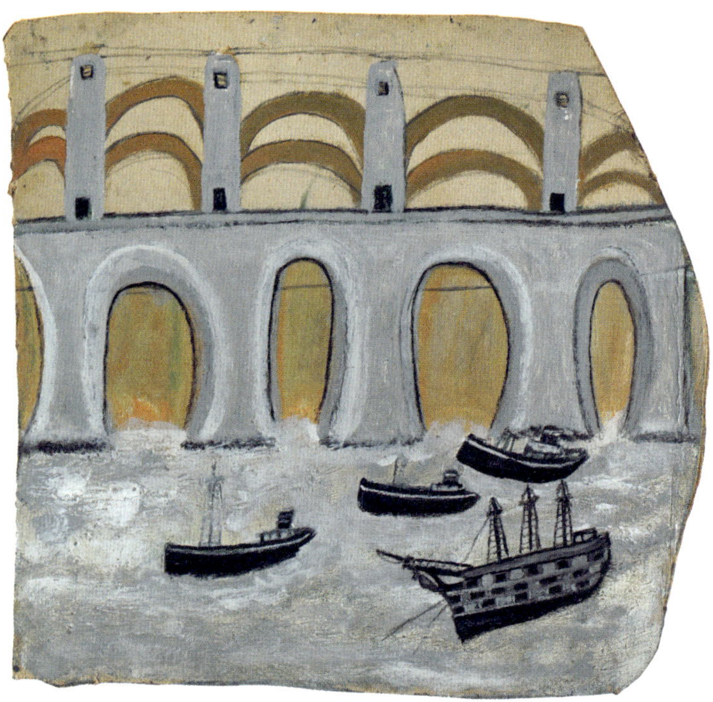

Boats Before a Great Bridge (Royal Albert Bridge?) c.1935–7
Oil paint on card 36.7 × 39.2

that he was not new to prolonged and demanding voyages.

Having returned to Cornwall, he exchanged the ocean for inshore fishing around the coastal waters of Cornwall and Britain, primarily aboard luggers following the pilchard, herring and mackerel seasons, mixing this with general labouring work. One reason for this shift was that just before setting sail on *The Pride of the West*, Wallis had married Susan Ward, a widow twenty-one years his senior. Their first child had been born and died while Alfred was at sea, and a daughter born in 1879 also died in childhood the following year.

Around 1885, less than a decade after his return, Wallis moved from Penzance to St Ives, establishing himself there as a marine scrap merchant. As his brother had a similar business in Penzance, where Alfred had often helped out when not at sea, it seems likely that the owner of Charles's business had asked Alfred to set up another Marine Stores in St Ives. Alfred's business was established by 1887, and by 1898 had moved to a building with a frontage directly on the harbour front. Six years later he joined the Salvation Army, following the lead of his wife who had been associated with it while living in Penzance. By all accounts, Wallis was as industrious as he was God-fearing and the Marine Stores appeared to prosper.[3] His closure of the business in 1912 is often linked to the changes affecting the fishing industry at the time – it was contracting, in part because of the shifting reliance from sail to steam – yet his retirement may also have something to do with his and his wife's ages. In 1912 Wallis was fifty-seven but Susan seventy-eight, and they had already moved to the cottage he had bought a few years earlier at 3 Back Road West. On retirement, Susan drew a pension and Alfred continued working, doing odd jobs, labouring (he helped build military housing in St Ives during the First World War), and also continuing to make and sell pink ice cream, as well as sandwiches, toy windmills and lemonade.

Susan died in June 1922, aged eighty-eight. Following her funeral, which was conducted by the Salvation Army, Alfred was left alone. He became increasingly isolated and, only two or three years later, probably in 1925, he started to paint, as he later described, 'for company' (though it is known that he also drew while in the Marine Stores).[4] According to the account given to the artist Sven Berlin by the watchmaker Mr Edwards, whose shop on Fore Street Wallis regularly visited, one day

Wallis entered the shop, saying, 'Aw! I dono how to pass away time. I think I'll do a bit a *paintin*' think I'll *draw* a bit.' Having first bought two watercolour brushes from a nearby shop, he then 'went to the paint shop in the Digey, Mr Burrell, and bought some ordinary house paint.'[5] He continued painting and drawing until shortly before his death just over fifteen years later.

In his paintings Wallis recalled particular memories of his working life as well as the sights that were starting to change markedly: the ships and boats he had sailed in, the coastlines and harbours he once knew well, the landscape he had walked through with his cart moving salvage between Penzance and St Ives. His paintings describe a working world, yet Wallis ignored this aspect himself when describing them; he preferred to concentrate on memory, pointing out how his paintings showed things and a way of life that no longer existed. When more up-to-date imagery surfaces – aeroplanes, airships, a cruise liner – these seem like interruptions to the world he conjured up.

In the summer of 1928, three years after Wallis had begun to paint, Ben and Winifred Nicholson were holidaying in Cornwall along with Christopher Wood and his girlfriend Frosca Munster – first, in late July, at Feock in Pill Creek, not far from Falmouth off the Carrick Roads, then moving to St Ives itself in August. Ever since he had visited the Nicholsons in Cumberland earlier that year, Wood had been attempting to distance himself from the urbanity of the Parisian art world he had previously been moving through (as typified by his friendship with Jean Cocteau). Ben Nicholson had been growing similarly disenchanted throughout the 1920s with the slick sophistication with which he associated his father William Nicholson's work, gradually

stepping back from it in a process he described as 'wanting to get right back to the beginning and then take one step forward at a time on a firm basis'.[6] Both artists, then, were more than ready for the effect of encountering Wallis's painting, which they did on a visit to St Ives shortly before they moved there from Feock. Nicholson's account of this momentous event is vivid:

this was an exciting day, for not only was it the first time I saw St Ives, but on the way back from Porthmeor Beach we passed an open door in Back Road West and through it saw some paintings of ships and houses on odd pieces of paper and cardboard nailed up all over the wall, with particularly large nails through the smallest ones. We knocked on the door and inside found Wallis, and the paintings we got from him then were the first he made.[7]

What made Wallis so important to Ben and Winifred Nicholson and Christopher Wood in 1928 was the manner in which he distilled his experience into his work – revealed to them as an authentically produced aesthetic truth. For Ben Nicholson in particular, Wallis's paintings affirmed the direction that he had taken, away from the depictive realities typified by his father's work and towards the spiritual essence of his subject. This move was reflective of his and his wife's involvement with Christian Science in seeking to create what the collector Helen Sutherland had described the previous year as paintings that originate 'with the spirit, the inward life, and this creates its own image in the world of appearances'.[8] The Tate Gallery curator Jim Ede wrote about Nicholson's work, also in 1927, in similar terms, describing its 'childlike simplicity' and the paintings' realisation as 'the direct manifestation of an inner life'.[9]

Wood had little sympathy with the Nicholsons' allegiance to Christian Science, but Wallis's paintings exerted a similar pull on him, and they had a much more tangible effect on his painting. Once the Nicholsons left St Ives in October, Wood remained there a few more weeks and visited Wallis regularly – visits that were catalogued in letters to Winifred Nicholson: 'More and more influence de Wallis, not a bad master though'[10] and 'I know all my boats and things without making drawings anymore … I see him [Wallis] each day for a second.'[11] By 'knowing all my boats', Wood indicated he was freed by Wallis's example of painting from memory, which contributed to the growing spontaneity and boldness of his handling. He also followed Wallis's example regarding materials by using a smaller range of colours and often exchanging oils for enamel paints.

The simplifications and distortions Wood and Nicholson found in Wallis's paintings were echoed in their paintings. What was crucial for them, however, was the authenticity of Wallis's expression, which communicated a knowledge and memory of experience rather than literal depiction. Wallis's paintings of St Ives are more often than not composite views of the terrain between land and sea, experienced and then brought back to life by memory and paint rather than just objectively transcribed and recorded. It was this concretising of experience that Nicholson and Wood were reaching for – and that characterised what Nicholson understood to be the 'unselfconscious', 'genuine', 'direct and vital' expression of 'primitive' painting, as he explained over thirty years later:

A primitive painter … will have worked on any form in which he was interested in order to try to realise in this some experience, something not on the surface but as deeply embedded in the material as in himself. This instinctive and unspoilt approach has a natural conviction and is capable of producing something even more actual than the original experience.[12]

Wallis's approach to painting didn't alter markedly from the moment he started in 1925 with some watercolour brushes and house paint from Mr Burrell's paint shop on the Digey. He continued using a small range of colours – usually house paint or marine paint – and painted on whatever surface was to hand, such as table tops, chests or jugs, but especially on packaging cardboard given him by the local grocer Mr Baughan and others. Nicholson described Wallis's preparation:

He would cut out the top and bottom of an old cardboard box, and sometimes the four sides into irregular shapes, using each shape as the key to the movement in his painting, and using the colour and texture of the board as the key to its colour and texture. When the painting was completed, what remained of the original board, a brown, a grey, a white or a green board, sometimes in the sky, sometimes in the sea, or perhaps in a field or a lighthouse, would be as deeply experienced as the remainder of the painting. He used very few colours.[13]

As Nicholson explained to Jim Ede after Wallis's death: 'I don't think a good Wallis is representational, it is simply REAL.'[14]

In one respect, Wallis's pictures are autobiographical factual records. Yet as representations they were not straightforwardly descriptive, but instead made to fit his memory as events made tangible. Ede wrote tellingly about Wallis's work that 'Each painting is to him a re-living, a re-presenting, achieved unconsciously in the act of painting, but vividly conscious in its factual awareness.'[15] Yet, for Ede, this 'factual awareness' arguably referred to the material nature of the painting rather than the factual content of the imagery and what it could tell us about Wallis's life. Living alone, Wallis was recalling his life by painting the places he knew – the North Atlantic Ocean, St Ives and St Ives Bay, Mount's Bay, Plymouth, Saltash and Devonport, the estuaries near where he fished latterly, and the landscape he would have laboured in or travelled through with his donkey and cart collecting scrap. He painted, too, boats he had sailed and worked on or among, from four-masters, schooners and barques to small mackerel luggers and gaff-rigged sloops; whether or not they were numbered and named, he knew them well: the *Belle Aventure*, the *Flying Scud* lugger out of Newlyn that he fished on or the Lowestoft fishing fleet he encountered chasing for mackerel. Some paintings also express his religious beliefs, from the fish in the sea to visions of Noah's Ark.

Wallis's memories are personally felt, but his work was also intended to be a record of a past that was vanishing or had already gone. In one letter, he wrote to Jim Ede: 'what i do mosley is what use to bee out of my own memery what we may never see again as thing are altered all together ther is nothin what ever do not look like what it was sence i can rember.'[16] The fishing fleets were diminished and the practice of seine net fishing for pilchards in St Ives Bay had ceased more than twenty years before Nicholson and Wood's encounter with Wallis in 1928. In this way, Wallis's paintings are an inscription into historical record, and his participation in this story is a key aspect of Sven Berlin's 1949 account of the artist's work and life, which mixes oral history with a romanticising interpretative approach to the book's subject.

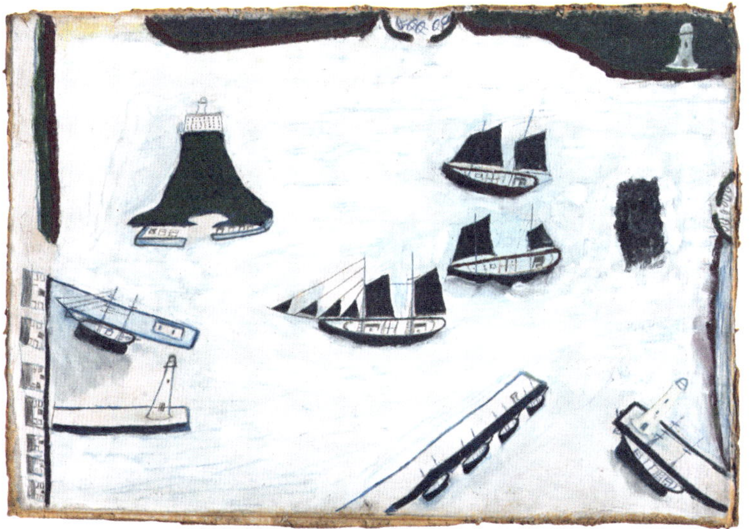

Mount's Bay with four lighthouses undated
Oil paint, crayon and graphite on card 44.5 × 65

There are two contrasting yet intertwined viewpoints to be taken on Wallis's work. On the one hand, it provided permission and affirmation in the late 1920s to moves being made by Ben Nicholson and Christopher Wood and those in their circle. Later, by the 1940s, its expressive authenticity offered a support for a broad sweep of modernist art (quite apart from coming to define the essential nature of art produced in St Ives for the subsequent thirty years or so). As the art historian and critic Alan Bowness suggested, Wallis 'was not an isolated and eccentric figure, but someone who was every bit as necessary to English painters as the Douanier Rousseau was necessary to Picasso and his friends. When art reaches an over-sophisticated stage, someone who can paint out of his experience with an unsullied and intense personal vision becomes of inestimable value.'[17] From another

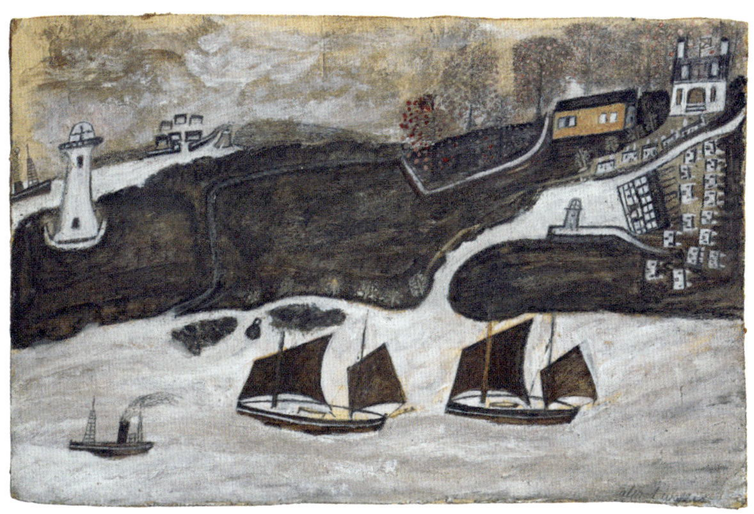

*Two ships and a steamer sailing past a port – Falmouth
and St Anthony Lighthouse* c.1931
Oil paint on card 26.3 × 40.9

perspective, however, Wallis's work provides a record of the devout working life of a widowed Cornish mariner from the late nineteenth century. This tension surrounding what Wallis chose to depict and what it meant to him and others became even more pronounced towards the end of his life and in the circumstances surrounding the production of the sketchbooks that this book reproduces.

A photograph of Ben Nicholson's Hampstead studio published in the 1934 book *Unit One* shows an array of his own paintings and prints, but hanging over the mantelpiece is Wallis's painting *Houses in St Ives* (Tate). Nicholson habitually displayed paintings by Wallis in his home and studio in Hampstead; however, although he continued to correspond with Wallis and bought or was given paintings, he only returned

twice to St Ives after 1928 – in March 1932 and in 1939. Having moved to Cornwall following the first bombing of London in 1939, he again started to see Wallis more frequently, often with Barbara Hepworth. In the more than ten years since their first meeting, however, Wallis's significance for Nicholson and his contemporaries, such as Adrian Stokes, had shifted markedly. In the late 1920s, Wallis's work had reflected and reinforced Nicholson's move towards a more naïve or 'primitive' way of painting that expressed truth and reality as he saw it. But by the time of the photograph in *Unit One*, Nicholson's artistic identity had changed so that ideals of truth and reality were now being expressed through the form of an ascetic purity found most typically in his series of *White Reliefs* after 1934, such as *1934 (relief)* 1934 (Tate), and his identification with the extreme abstraction and constructivism of international modernism – seemingly a world away from Wallis's pictured memories.

In 1938, the critic Sir Herbert Read had published an assessment of contemporary British art for the French magazine *Cahiers d'Art* that essentially pivoted between surrealism and abstraction. The inclusion of Wallis within this account made clear his significant position within British art's recent history – indeed, he was the first artist to be reproduced and addressed in Read's article – but he occupied a rather singular position. Read described Wallis's work as the innocent vision of a retired sailor, characterising him as an old man who had retained the eyes of an infant, but also, more significantly, as an artist who had produced a body of work that was completely indigenous ('purement indigène') and had absolutely no awareness of or interest in developments in art in Paris or elsewhere.[18] Although he remained an indicative exemplar of a particular approach to art embodying truth and experience in its naïve vision, Wallis was also by 1938 an anomaly. And yet for Nicholson, his renewed proximity to Wallis during the last three years of his life framed another shift in his work. Within a comparatively short time the spare, ascetic white purity of his *White Reliefs* and subsequent orthogonal abstract paintings gave way as the landscape of St Ives and still-life motifs explicitly made their way into his painting once more. As the historian Charles Harrison explained, 'Nicholson certainly did not represent St Ives in Wallis's terms, but perhaps his awareness of the *kinds* of attention signified in Wallis's paintings helped to determine how he himself thought about what he saw.'[19]

Nicholson's move to Cornwall, initially to Carbis Bay before finding a home and studio in St Ives itself, coincided with a shift in Wallis's health. Sven Berlin's account pinpoints an episode in 1936 or 1937 when he was knocked down by the mayor's car on the Digey: 'He was very badly shaken up and was never quite the same man afterwards. His age at that time was eighty-two … One cannot help noticing how oddly symbolic it was that our Ancient Mariner should be knocked down by a modern machine.'[20] Wallis wrote about this event to Ede in 1937, but also in a note to Mr Baughan the grocer, describing what he called in a further letter to Ede the following year 'nothin But Percuitin and gelecy'.[21] The physical and mental mockery he lists would have fuelled other paranoias and religious visions as well as his increased sense of isolation. By June 1941, unable to properly fend for himself, Wallis voluntarily went into the Madron Institution, a poorhouse outside Penzance. On one of his earliest visits to see Wallis there, Nicholson arrived with a copy of *Cahiers d'Art* to prove to the director and staff of the poorhouse that Wallis was a significant artist and should be properly looked after. He also explained that the painting by

Wallis that had been illustrated in Read's 1933 book *Art Now* – *St Ives Harbour* c.1932–3 – had entered the collection of the Museum of Modern Art New York the previous year.

After a month in bed, Wallis requested painting materials and was allowed to paint. Yet he was away not only from his home but also from the source of his materials – off-cuts of bits of cardboard and wood as well as household items – and the restricted colour range of everyday marine paints that he was accustomed to using. At first Stokes and Nicholson fetched paint and materials from his deserted and flea-ridden home, subsequently buying paints from Mr Burrell on the Digey – yet these Wallis refused to use, as he did some watercolours that he put away in a box and hid in his room. The materials he was given were a mix of the paints he had previously used and artists' materials on which he became unusually reliant – pencils and crayons, sketchbooks and enamel paints.

Sven Berlin recounts how Nicholson gave Wallis at this time a group of four sketchbooks. Three of these are reproduced here: the *Castle Book*, the *Grey Book* and the *Lion Book*. The fourth, the *Scrap Book*, is now unidentified; so too are at least two other scrapbooks known to have existed (although the pages have long been broken up and exist now as scattered leaves in individual collections), the *Universal Book* originally owned by Berlin and the *Derwent Book* that had been owned by the sculptor Denis Mitchell. Describing these books, Berlin explains:

A good deal of painting was done at Madron and some excellent drawings. The drawings were done mainly in greasy crayon – some in pencil. Nicholson had taken him four sketchbooks, which he filled on both sides of each page in a very short time. These are extremely interesting.

The use of brightly coloured crayon is new, as is the regular
shape of the paper he now had to work on. Where the *Lion Book*
and *Castle Book* are children's drawing books or scrapbooks made
up of cheap utility paper, the *Grey Book* is a hardback clothbound
artists' watercolour sketchbook manufactured by Roberson, and
probably accompanied the watercolours that Wallis rejected
and hid. The *Grey Book* is the only book of the three to be painted
using a green and black enamel or oil paint alongside pencil and
coloured crayon.

In only a few instances can Wallis's paintings be dated, and
given that his work was driven by the workings of memory,
it has never been possible to understand the course of that
memory as it unspooled from one work to the next. The mix
of different styles and ages of boat, the relationship of boats to
land and to isolated landmarks, and the repetition and variation
of particular subjects and views all speak to the retrieval,

through the pages of each book, of memories and experiences
that he had perpetually rehearsed in his painting over the
previous fifteen years or so – motifs from much earlier being
revisited in these drawings. The sequence of memory in these
sketchbooks doesn't seem to suggest any coherent narrative,
however – especially as the *Castle Book* has drawings in different
orientations, breaking with the idea of a sequence of one
drawing to the next.

One characteristic of a number of the pages in these
sketchbooks complicates Wallis's visualisation of the action of
his memory. These are not just composite views of boats and the
land from sea, but also conjure up composite chronologies where
different eras of sail and steam are mixed together. This is also
true of the *Grey Book*, where there also seems a greater sense of
consistency in how successive pages communicate a passing of
time by cataloguing the ships and boats in which Wallis sailed,
whether on the North Atlantic or inshore fishing.

The book ends with three mysterious drawings that may offer
an interpretation of Noah's Ark, or relate a religious gathering by
the shore, whether blessing or funeral. The first drawing in this
sequence shows a houseboat sited on a green plateau, perhaps a
Cornish equivalent to the Ark on Mount Ararat following the
subsiding of the flood; the next shows a valley or cliffside and
headland view of a congregation of people on top
of a hill and around its base with three tabernacle structures,
possibly an indication of survivors giving thanks following the
flood's aftermath. The last drawing shows an estuary landscape
of fields, emphasising a rebirth or renewed creation. Wallis was a
devout and religious man: on Sundays he would cover over any
of his paintings in his home and spend the day reading his family
Bible. Edwin Mullins, in his study of Wallis, makes reference to

one account where Wallis points to his representation of over-size fish, saying, 'That fish stands for all the fish that have ever swum – for all the fish that God ever put in the sea.' Mullins even suggests that 'the animals … were associated in his mind with the animals set free from the Ark. The notion of a world purged of sin by flood and repopulated with innocent creatures from the Ark is precisely the kind of ideal that a man with Wallis's puritanical views would be expected to hold.'[23] Barbara Hepworth remembered that on his painting table beside his paints and brushes and close to his right hand was Wallis's enormous Bible[24] – as he wrote to Nicholson: 'i Tell you what i am a Bible Keeper it is Red 3 hundreds sixty times a year By me and That is averyons Duity.'[25]

Wallis died on 29 August 1942, just over one year after he had entered Madron. The survival of the sketchbooks, and their indication of the strength and renewal of Wallis's creative powers during his time there, is bound up with what Berlin identified in the first line of his 1942 sketch of Wallis, published in *Horizon* shortly after the artist's death:

It is part of the incalculable crime of modern life that people still starve, still live in abject poverty. We have the Poor Law to guard these sad lives, it is true; but only those who have been forced to use this law know the inadequacy of the help it extends … To an artist this agony is tenfold, because of his increased consciousness of life and his innate sensitivity.[26]

Wallis was spared a pauper's grave through the quick action of his friends, as well as the £20 that he had saved to cover funeral expenses, and the ceremony was conducted by the Salvation Army as he had wished. Berlin's subsequent book,

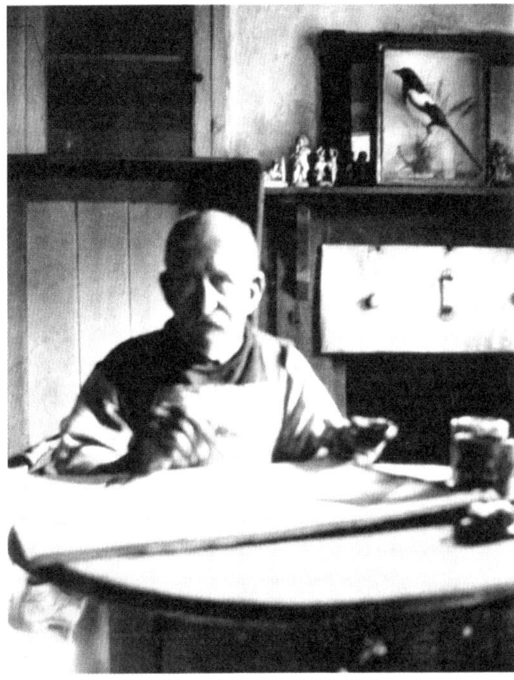

Photograph of Alfred Wallis, September 1928

Alfred Wallis: Primitive – conceived in wartime while Berlin was a conscientious objector, and then largely written in 1943 and 1944 after he joined the Royal Artillery, but not published until 1949 – was as much a labour of respect and love as the tiles, designed by Bernard Leach, that cover Wallis's grave.

Berlin's book starts with a movingly elegiac poem by the Scottish poet W.S. Graham, 'The Voyages of Alfred Wallis', which relates, in the manner of old English myth, the passage of Wallis's soul to safe harbour, 'keelheaved to Heaven'. Berlin had commissioned the poem from Graham – they had become friendly following his demobilisation – and it was written quickly in the early summer of 1945. It is a poem of ascension and resurrection, finely attuned to Berlin's account of the 'tragedy and glory of a life that was wholly sincere and valuable from the beginning: the story of a mind of genius endeavouring to grope its way to the light through the darkness of ignorance, extreme economic pressure, and the tyranny of a primitive religion.'[27]

The sketchbooks are the final testimony of Wallis's memory of 'what we may never see again'; he ended his days in Madron, and with one of his paintings hanging in the Museum of Modern Art in New York:

His poor house blessed by very poverty's religious
Breakwater, his past house hung in foreign galleries …

What shipcry falls? The holy families of foam
Fall into wilderness and 'over the jasper sea'.
The gulls wade into silence. What deep seasaint
Whispered this keel out of its element?[28]

1   Sven Berlin, *Alfred Wallis: Primitive*, London 1949, p.16. Berlin suggests that Wallis had one brother and two sisters and that the sisters both emigrated to Australia. He also repeats a statement made by Wallis to Ben Nicholson that he had twelve brothers and sisters – all supposedly buried along with his father and mother in Devonport Cemetery.
    Following the publication of Berlin's book, which included stories from family, friends and neighbours, Dr Roger Slack carried out interviews in the 1960s with St Ives residents who remembered Wallis; excerpts from these interviews have appeared in subsequent studies, most notably in Edwin Mullins, *Alfred Wallis: Cornish Primitive Painter*, London 1967. More recently, Peter Barnes carried out exhaustive archival research that both corrected and confirmed elements of these earlier accounts; his findings – published as *Alfred Wallis and his Family: Fact and Fiction*, St Ives 1997 – have fed into the two key subsequent studies, most notably Matthew Gale, *Alfred Wallis*, London 1998 and Robert Jones, *Alfred Wallis: Artist and Mariner*, revised edn, Hayle 2006. I have relied here, to varying degrees, on each of these accounts.
2   Berlin 1949, p.16. This claim, however, cannot be completely verified.
3   Berlin 1949, p.45, also suggests that during the 'first five seasons of his life in St Ives he continued to do coastal fishing on boats called the *Two Sisters* and *The Faithful*'. However, there is scant documentary evidence to support this, and it might have been hard to combine running a successful marine store with the demands of coastal fishing.
4   Jones 2006, p.122.
5   Berlin 1949., p.61.
6   Ben Nicholson, letter to Charles Harrison, Nov. 1966. Cited in Charles Harrison, 'Abstract Painting in Britain in the Early 1930's', *Studio International*, April 1967, p.186.
7   Ben Nicholson, 'Alfred Wallis: II', *Horizon*, vol.VII, no.37, Jan. 1943, p.50.
8   Helen Sutherland, 'Ideas', in *Stoneware pottery by W. Staite Murray and paintings by Ben Nicholson, Christopher Wood*, exh. cat., Beaux Arts Gallery, London, April 1927, unpag.
9   H.S. Ede, 'Ben Nicholson, Winifred Nicholson and William Staite Murray', *Artwork*, vol.4, no.16, Winter 1928, pp. 262, 267.
10 Quoted in Winifred Nicholson, *Kit*, typescript memoir, p.26. Tate Gallery Archive 753/100.
11 Ibid., p.28.
12 Ben Nicholson, 'Artist's Statement', in David Baxandall, *Ben Nicholson*, London 1962, unpag.
13 Nicholson 1943, p.50.
14 Ben Nicholson, letter to H.S. Ede, dated 29 Aug. 1942, Kettle's Yard Archive.
15 H.S. Ede : 'Two painters in Cornwall Alfred Wallis and Christopher Wood', World *Review*, March 1945, reprinted Elizabeth Fisher and Andrew Nairne, *Alfred Wallis, Ships and Boats*, exh. cat., Kettle's Yard, Cambridge 2012, p.36.
16 Alfred Wallis, letter to H.S. Ede, dated 6 April 1935, Kettle's Yard Archive.
17 Alan Bowness, 'Introduction', *Alfred Wallis*, exh. cat. Arts Council, Tate Gallery, London (and tour) 1968, unpag.
18 Herbert Read, 'L'Art Contemporain en Angleterre', *Cahiers d'Art*, no.1–2, 1938, p.31.
19 Charles Harrison, 'The Modern, the Primitive and the Picturesque', *Alfred Wallis, Christopher Wood, Ben Nicholson*, exh. cat., Scottish Arts Council, Edinburgh 1987, p.14.
20 Berlin 1949, p.85.
21 Alfred Wallis, letter to H.S. Ede, dated 27 July 1938, Kettle's Yard Archive.
22 Berlin 1949, p.114.
23 Mullins 1967, pp.88, 92.
24 See Barbara Hepworth, 'Icons of the Sea – Recollections of Alfred Wallis', *The Listener*, 20 July 1968.
25 Alfred Wallis to Ben Nicholson, undated fragment, Tate Gallery Archive 8717/1/2/5268
26 Sven Berlin, 'Alfred Wallis: I', *Horizon*, vol.VII, no.37, Jan. 1943, p.41.
27 Berlin 1949, p.9.
28 W.S. Graham, 'The Voyages of Alfred Wallis', in ibid., p.13.

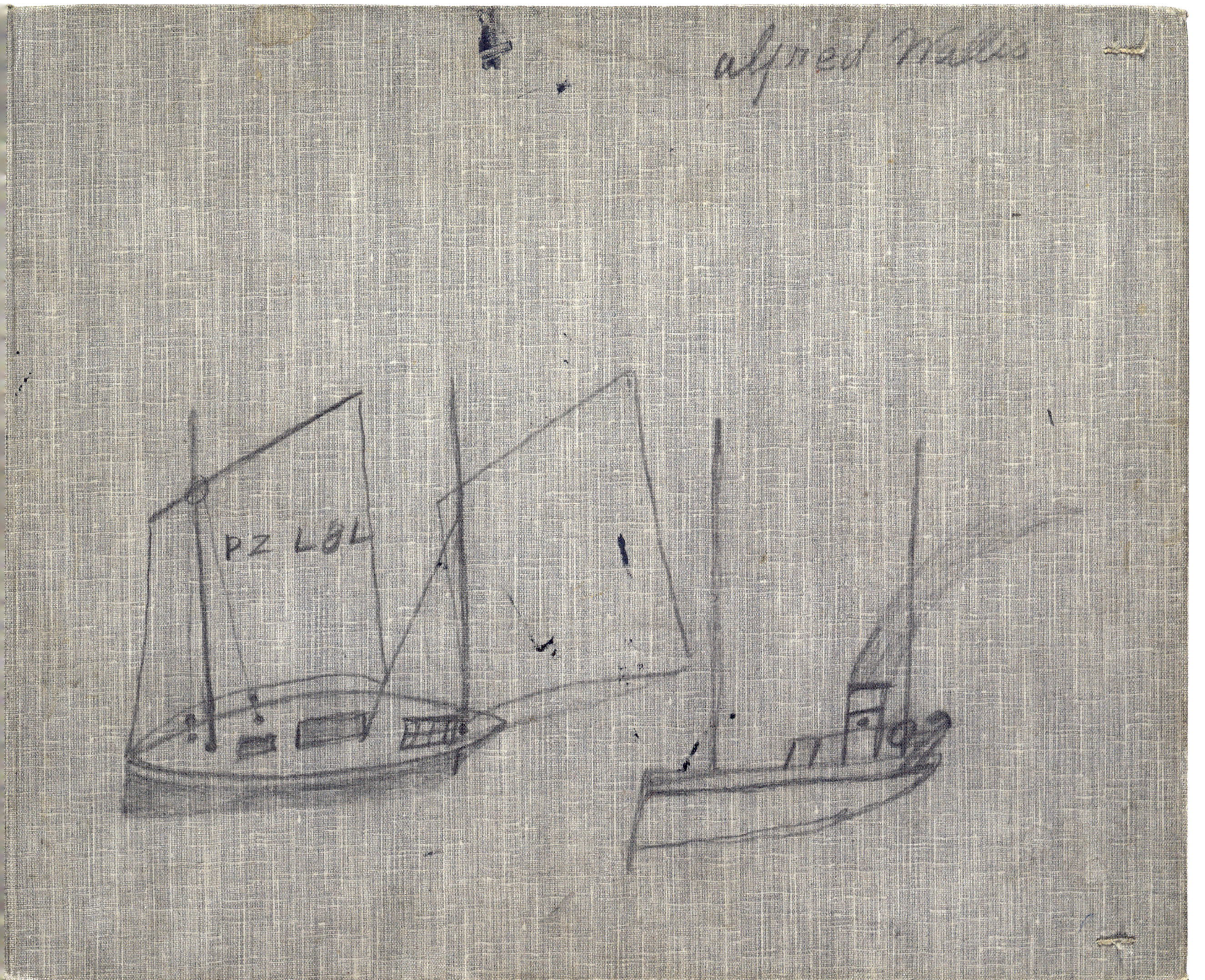
alfred Wallis
PZ L8L

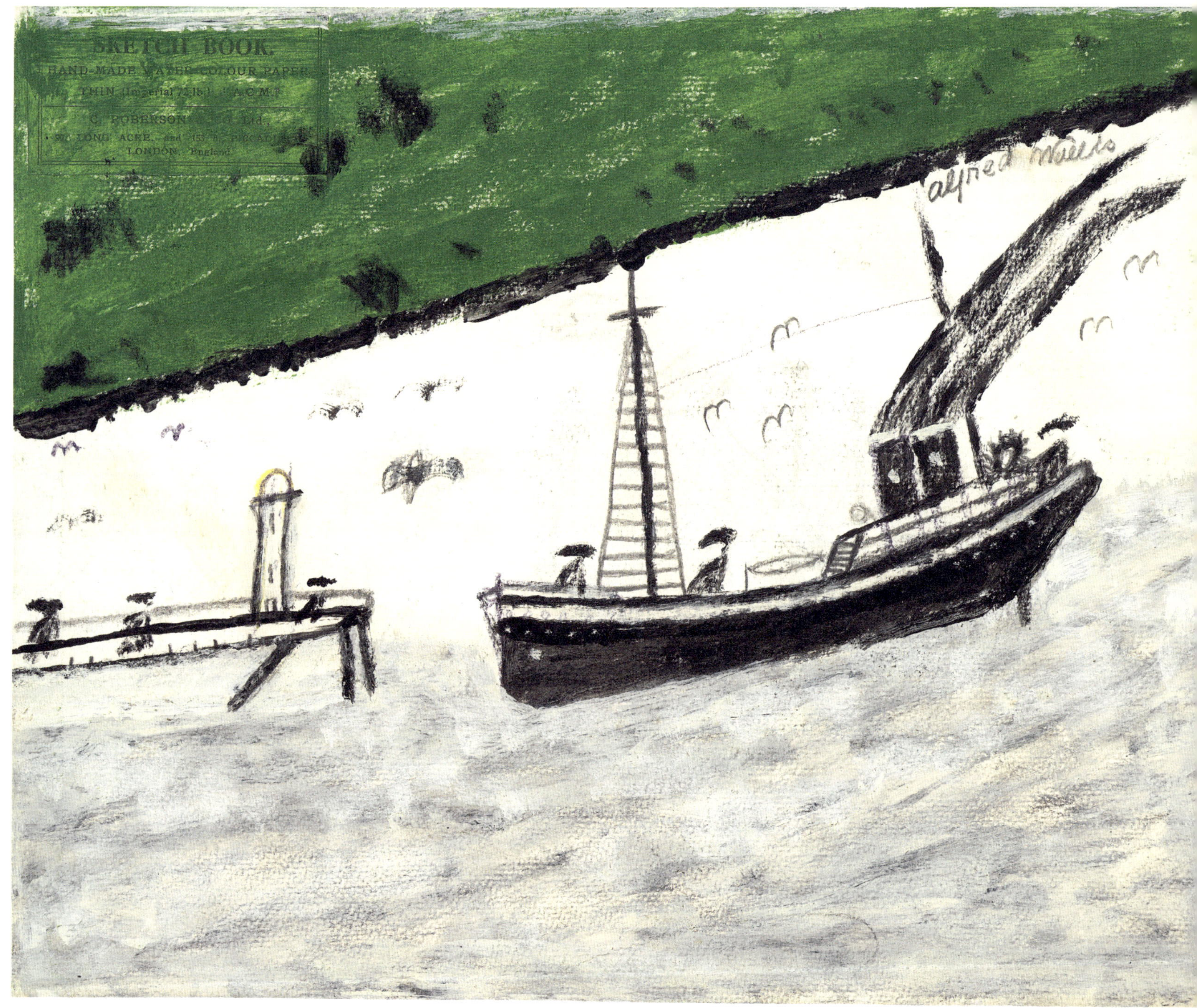

SKETCH BOOK.
HAND-MADE WATER COLOUR PAPER
THIN (Imperial 72 lb)   A.C.M.P.
C. ROBERSON & Co. Ltd
99 LONG ACRE, and 154 PICCADILLY
LONDON, England
alfred wallis

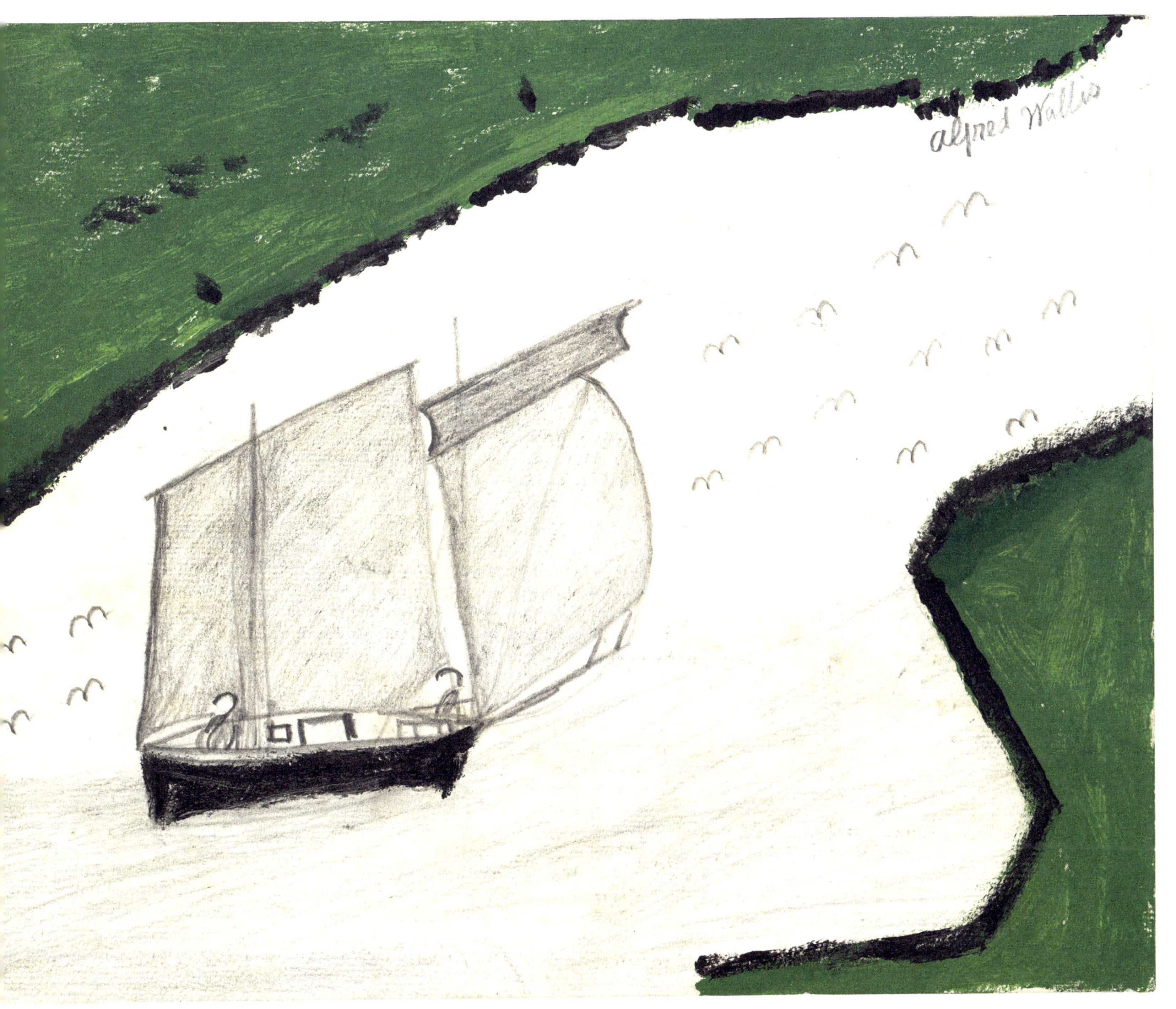

alfred wallis

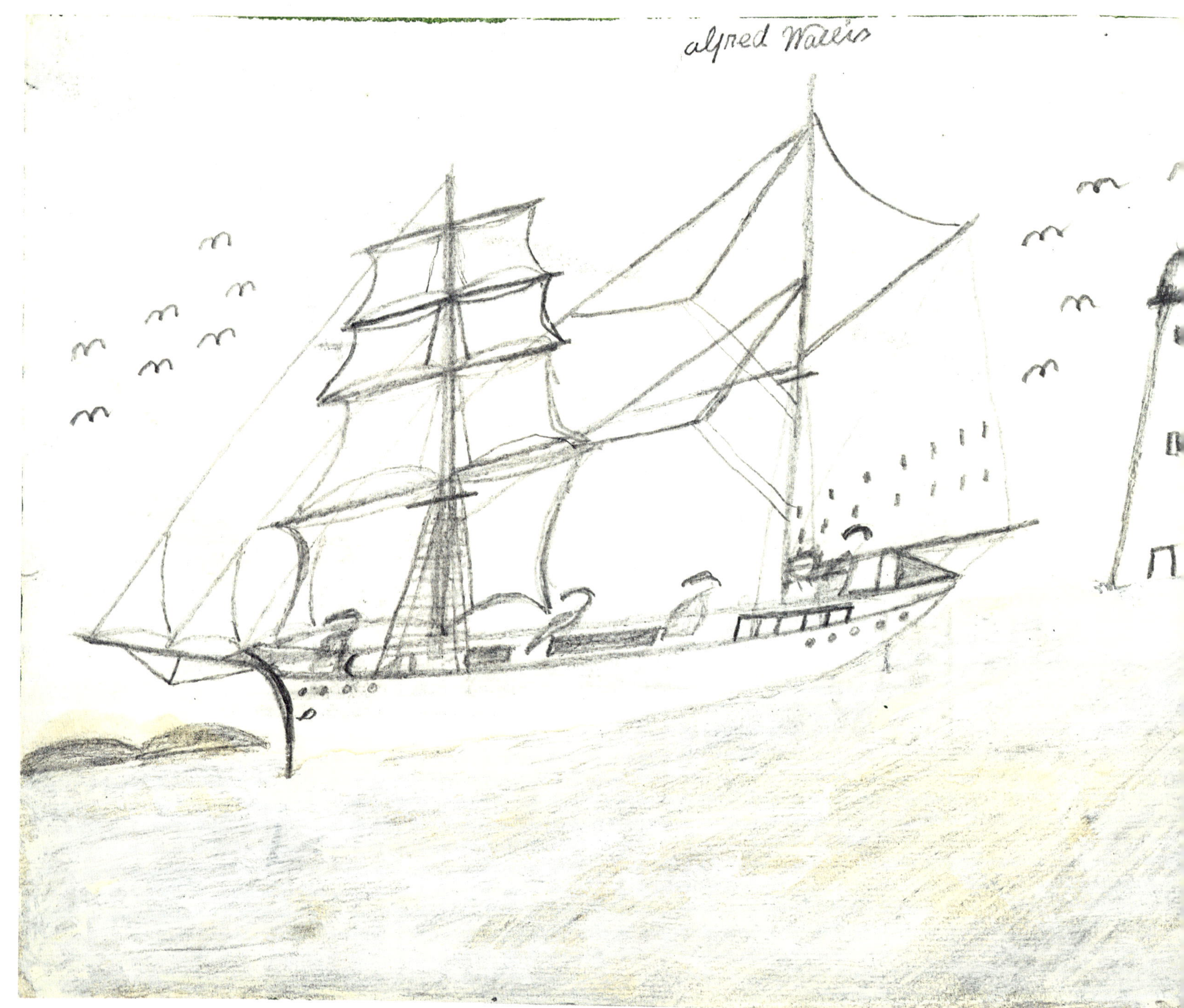

alfred Wallis

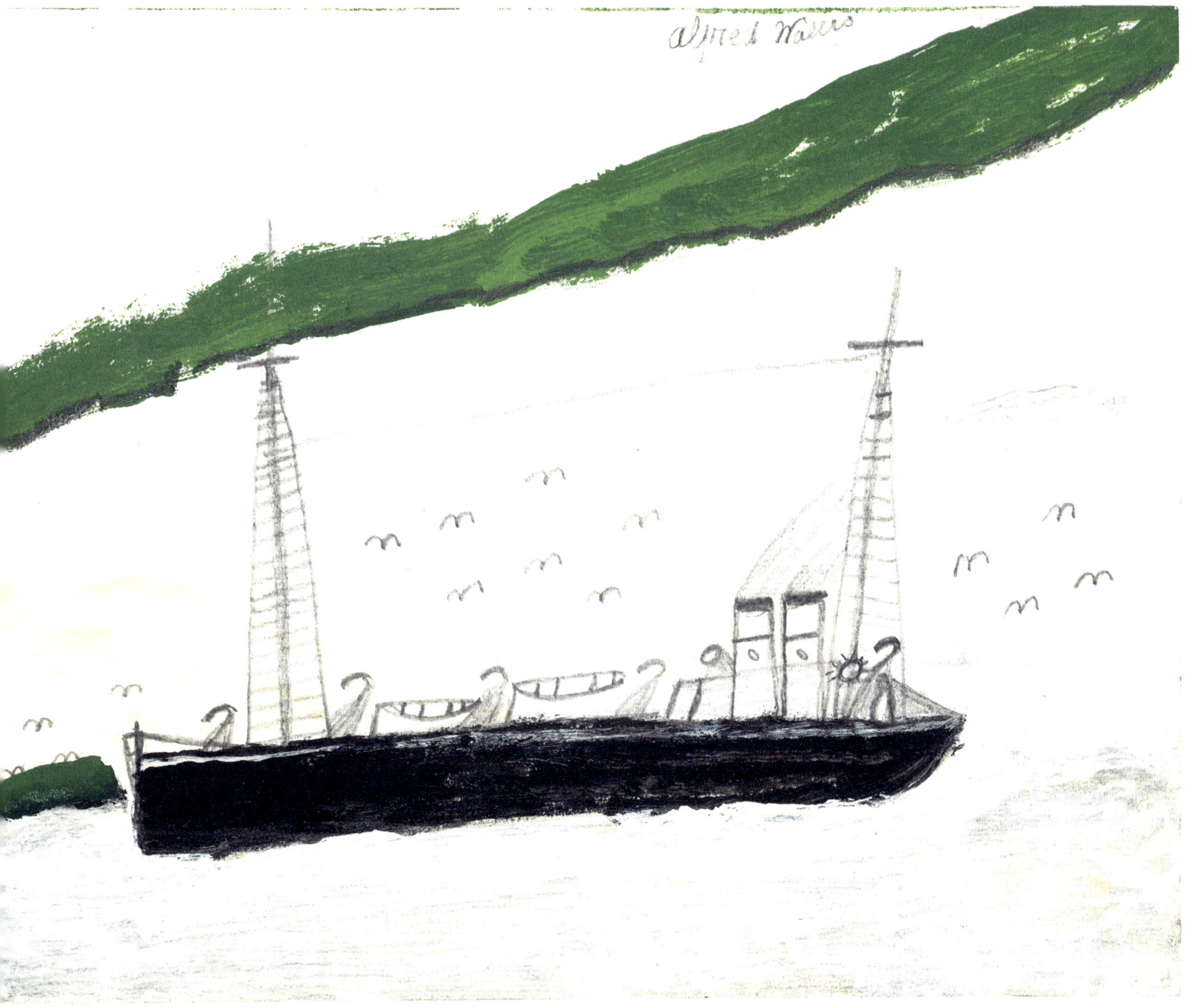
alfred wallis

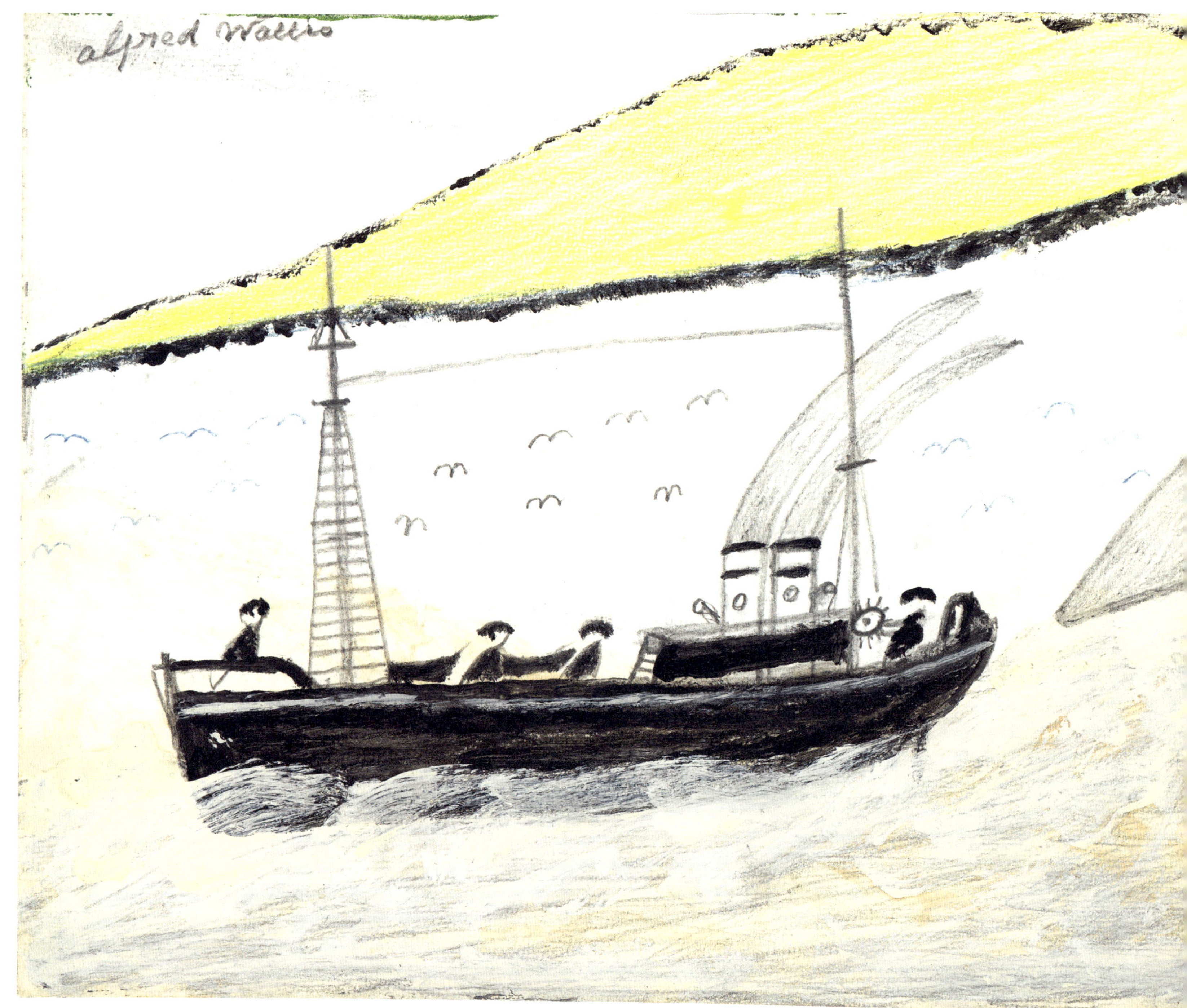

alfred wallis

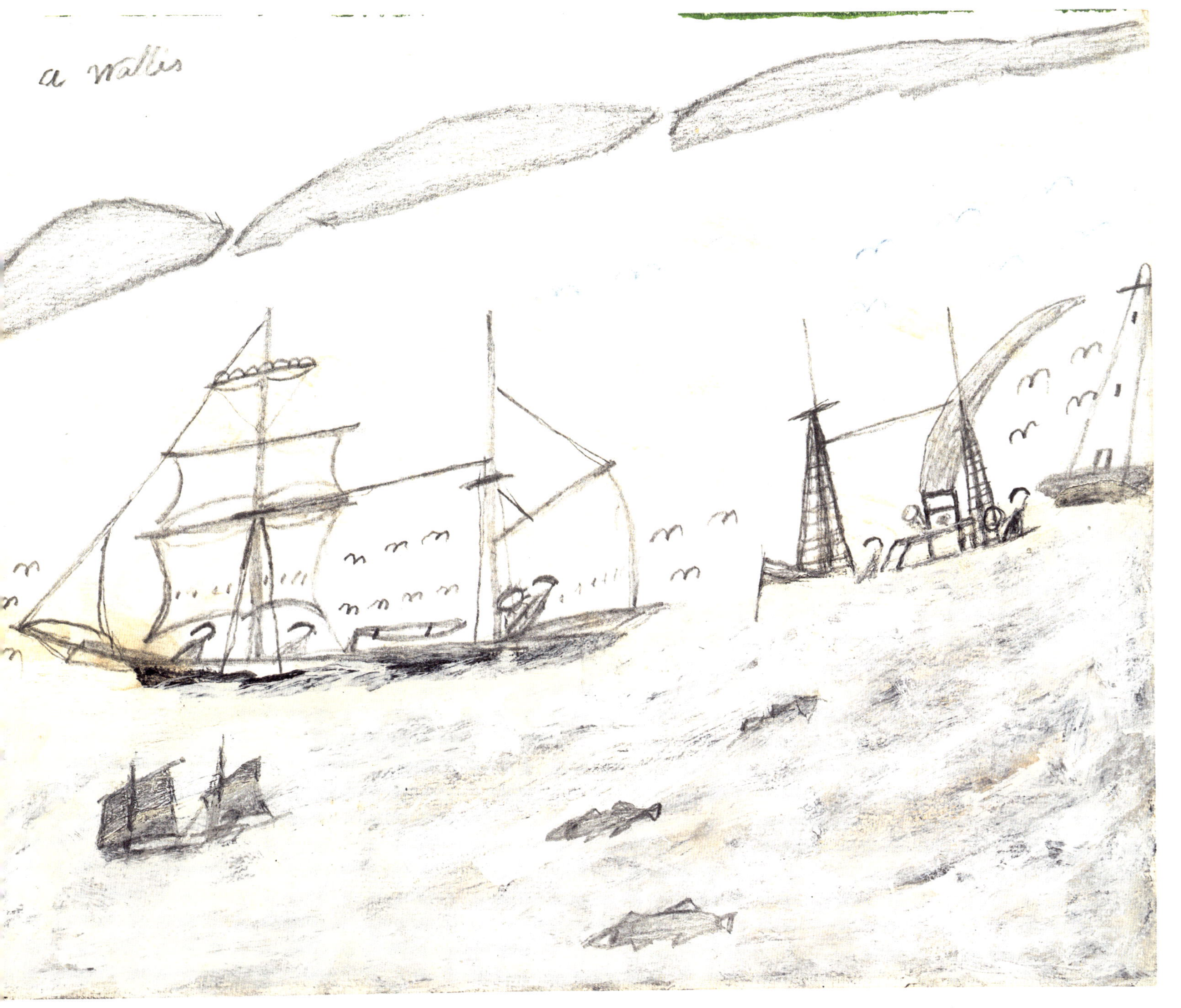

a Wallis

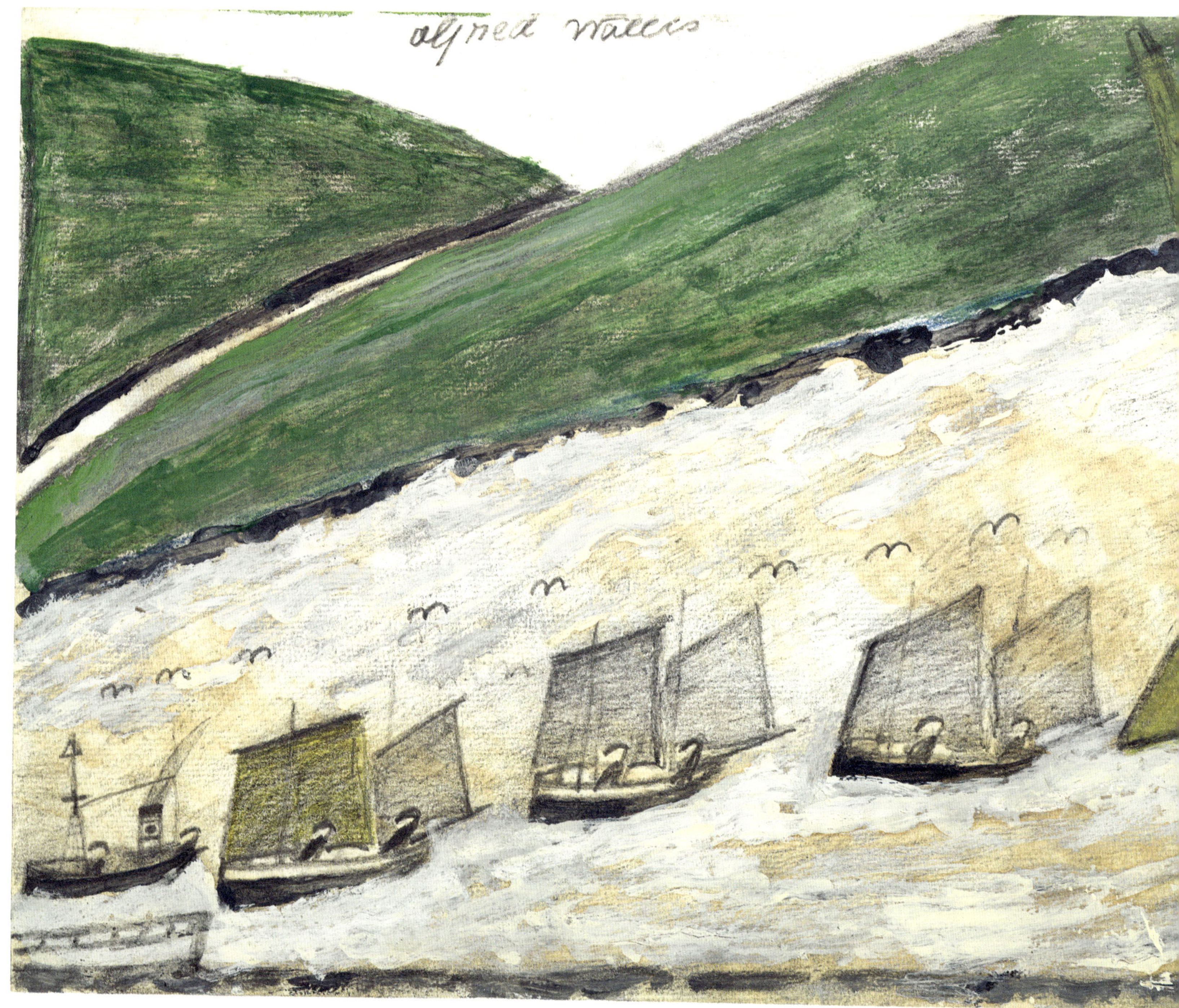
alfred wallis

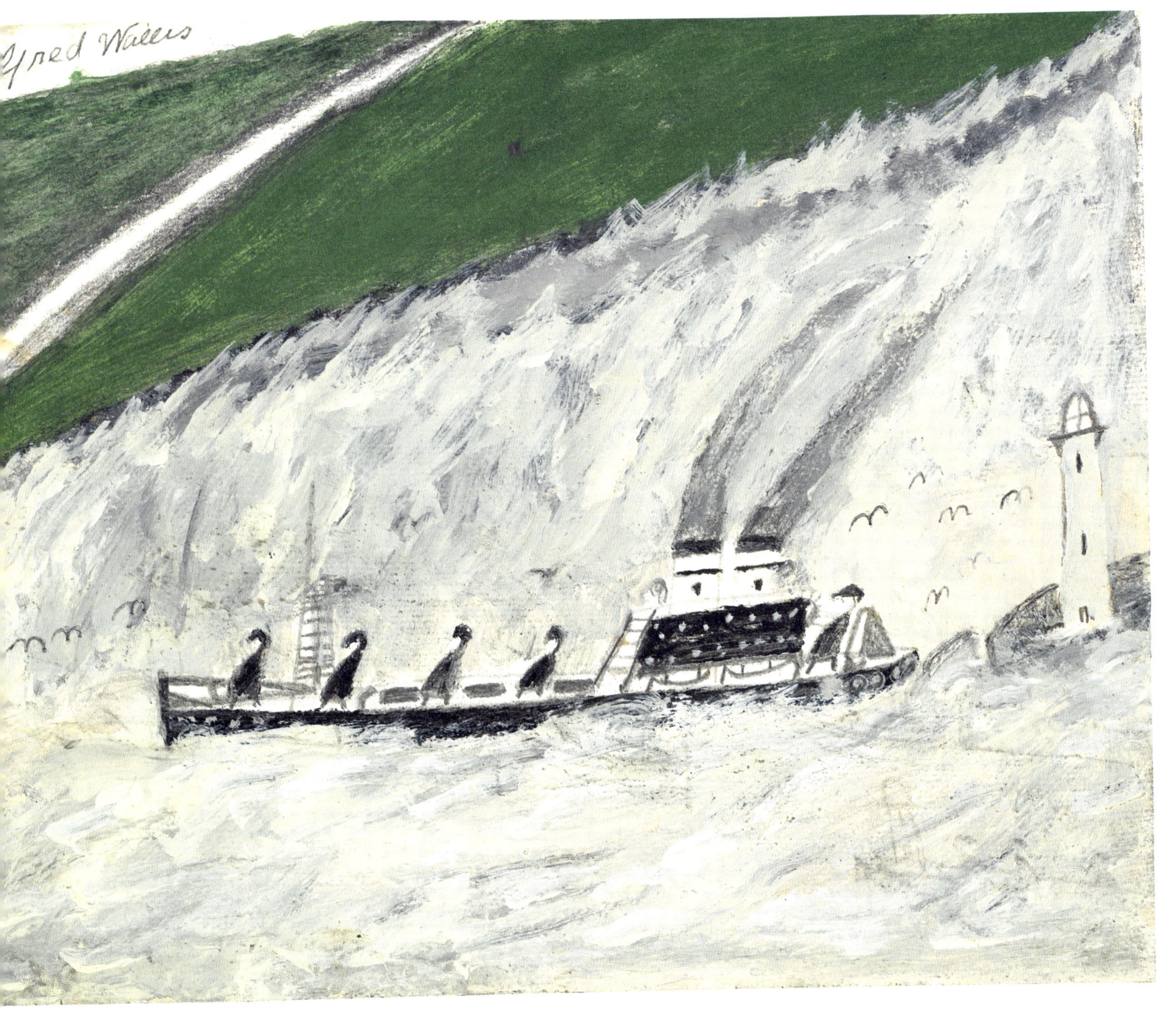

Alfred Wallis

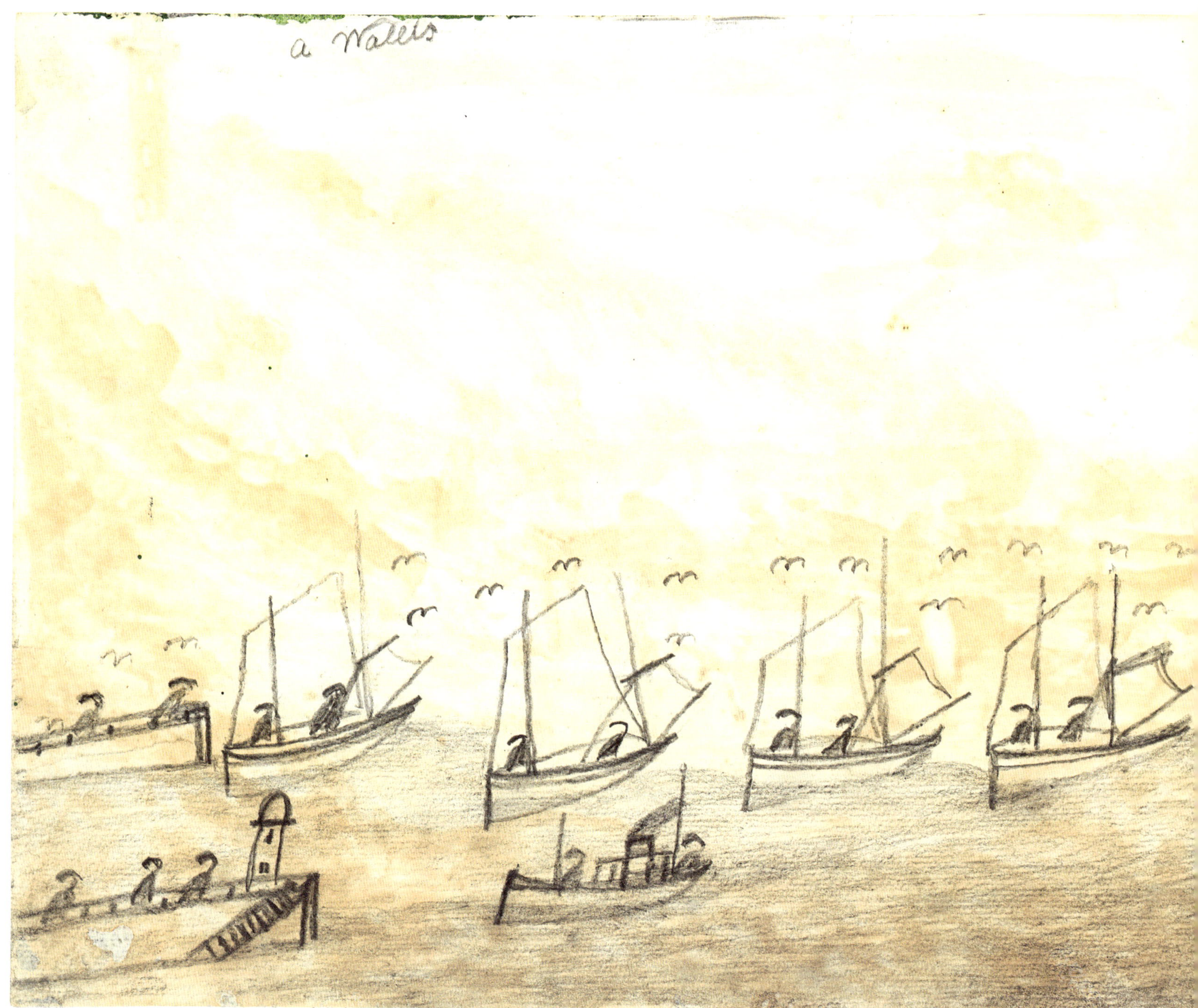
a Wallis

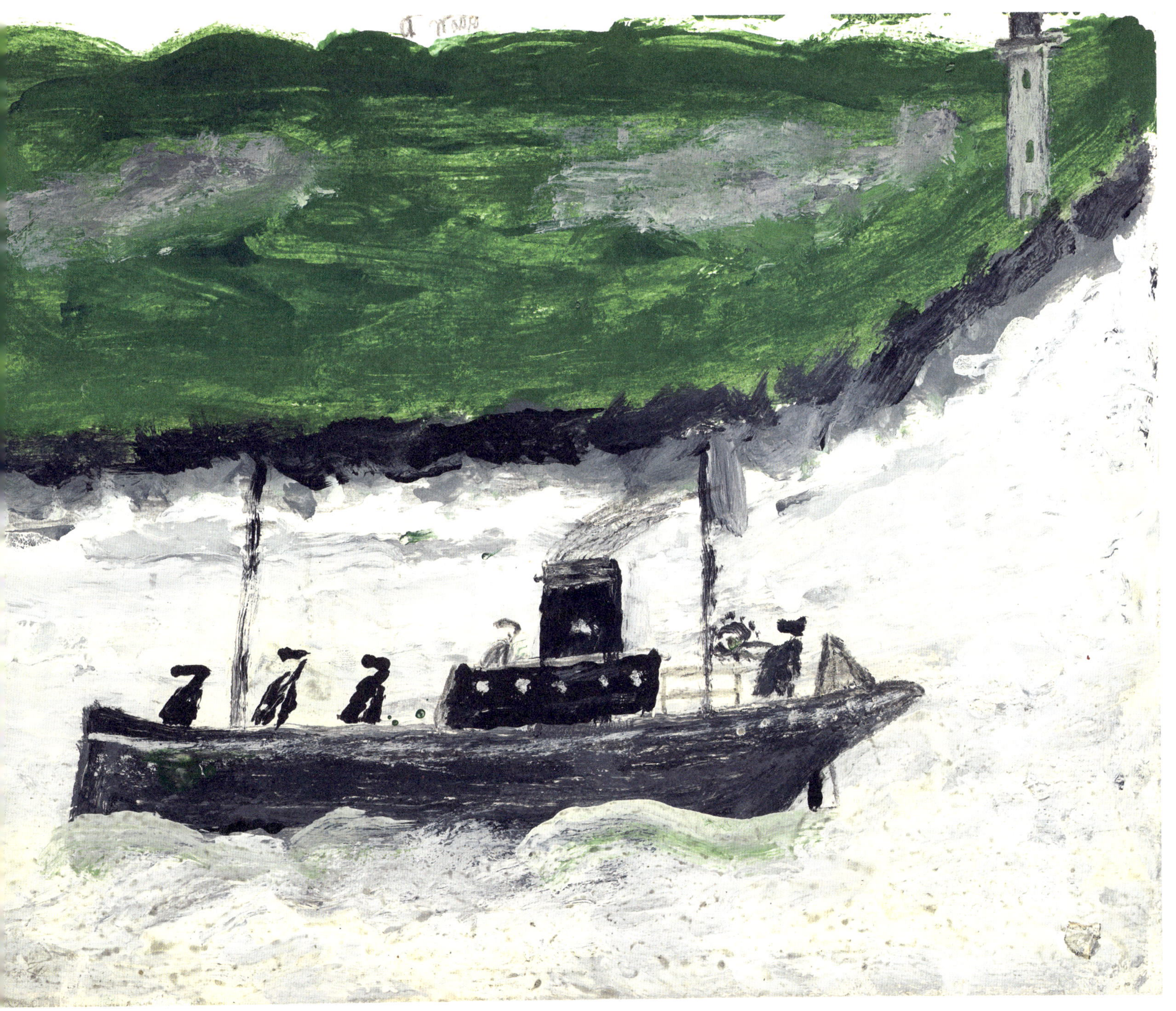

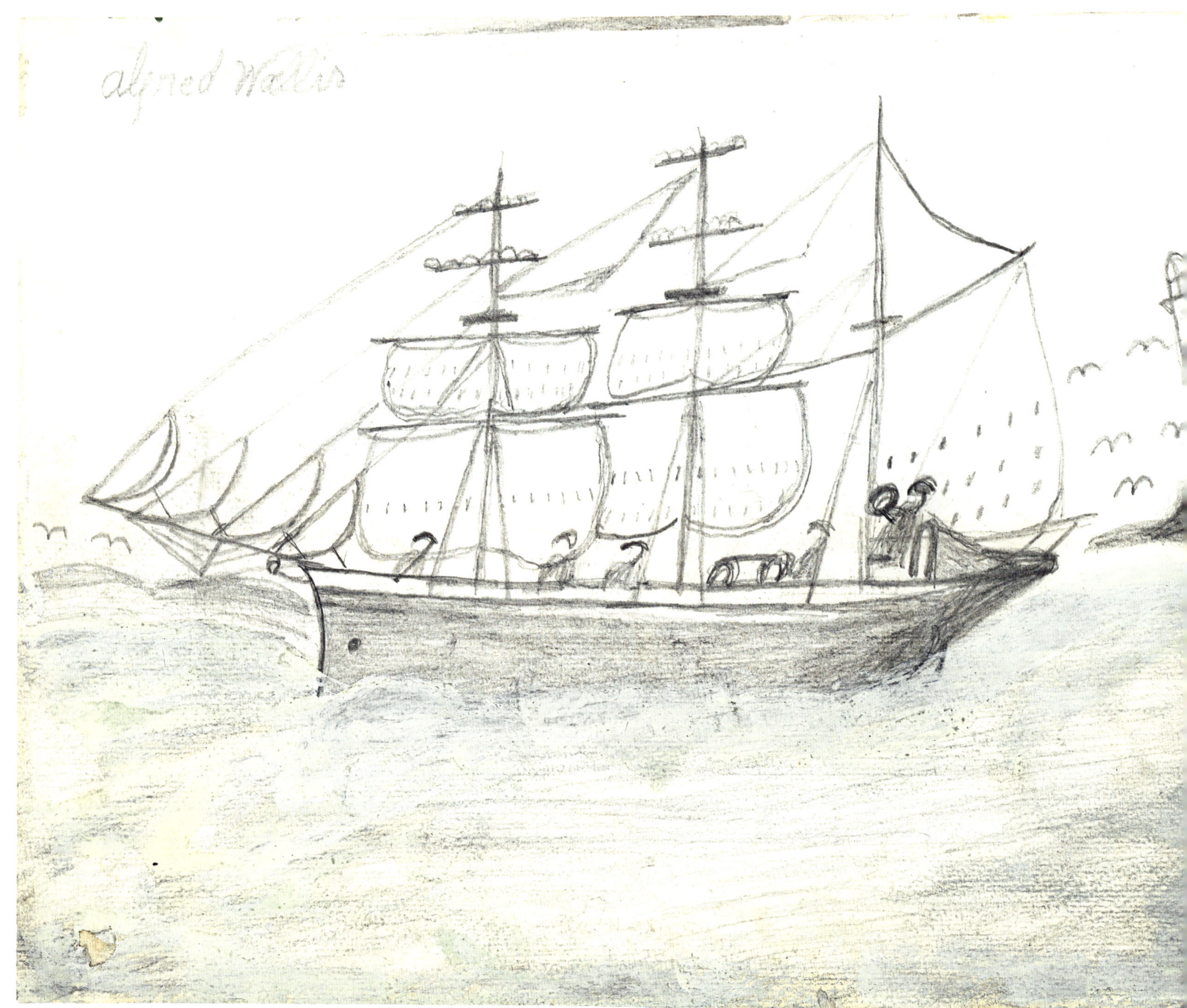
alfred wallis

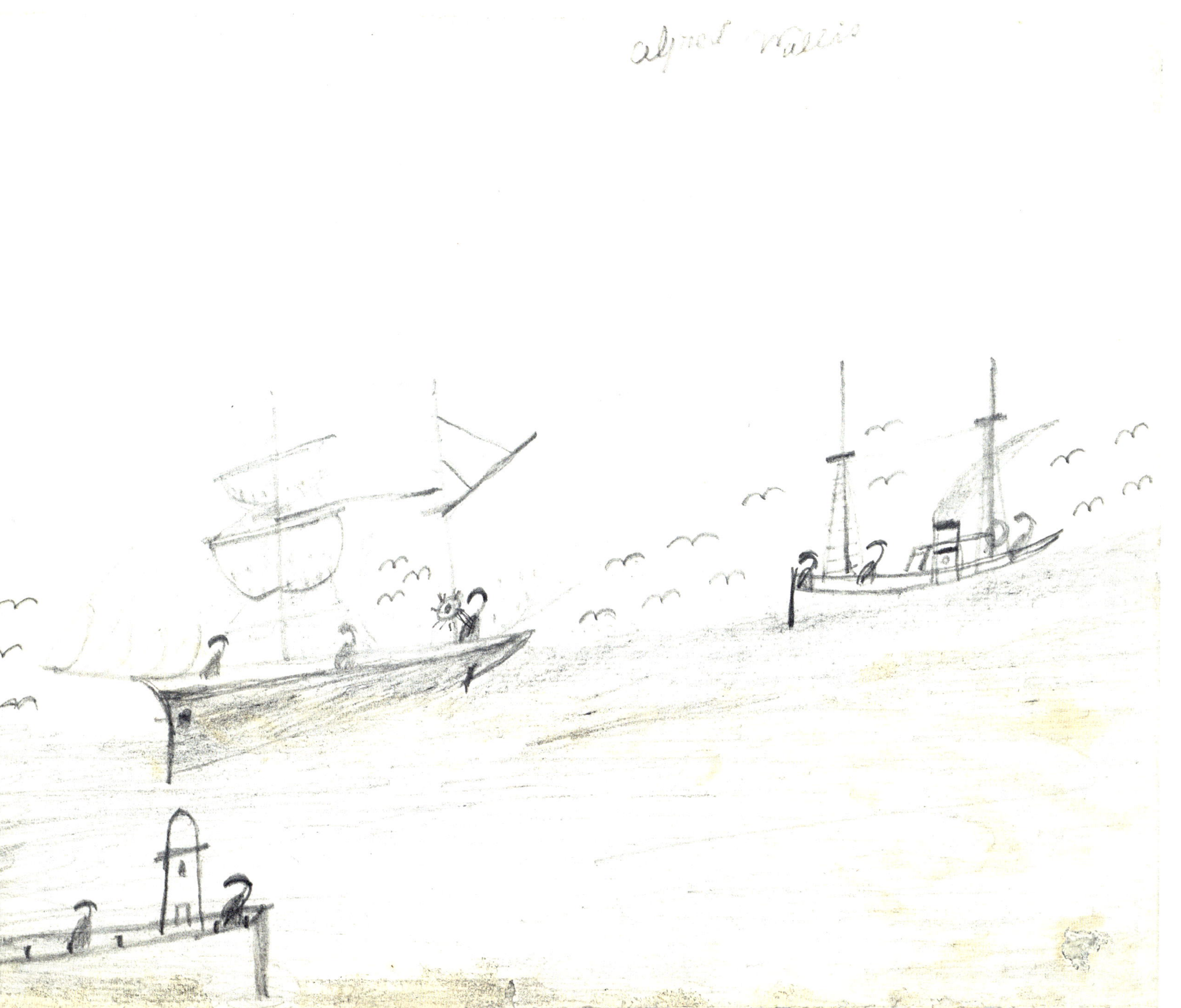

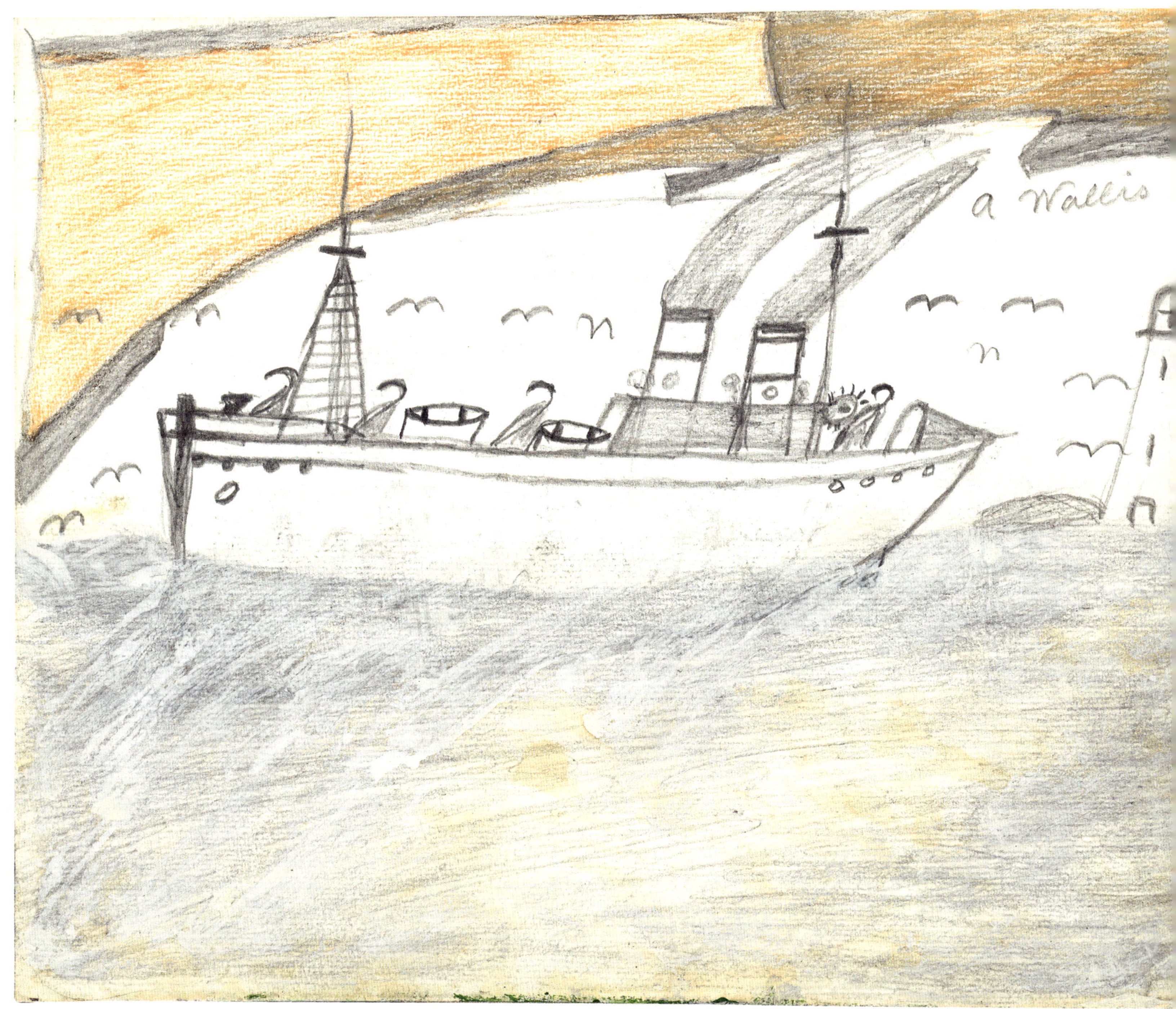
a Wallis

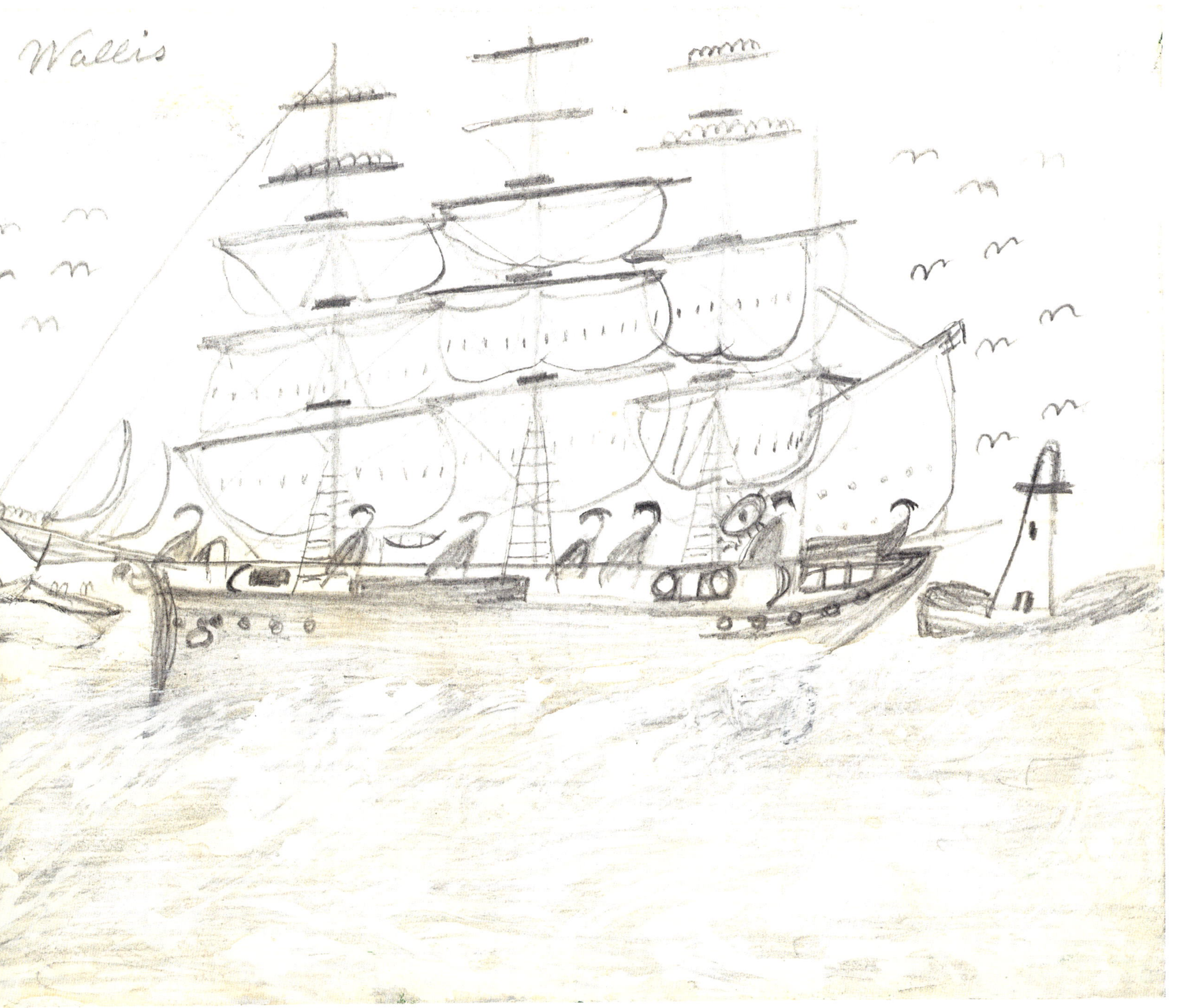

Wallis

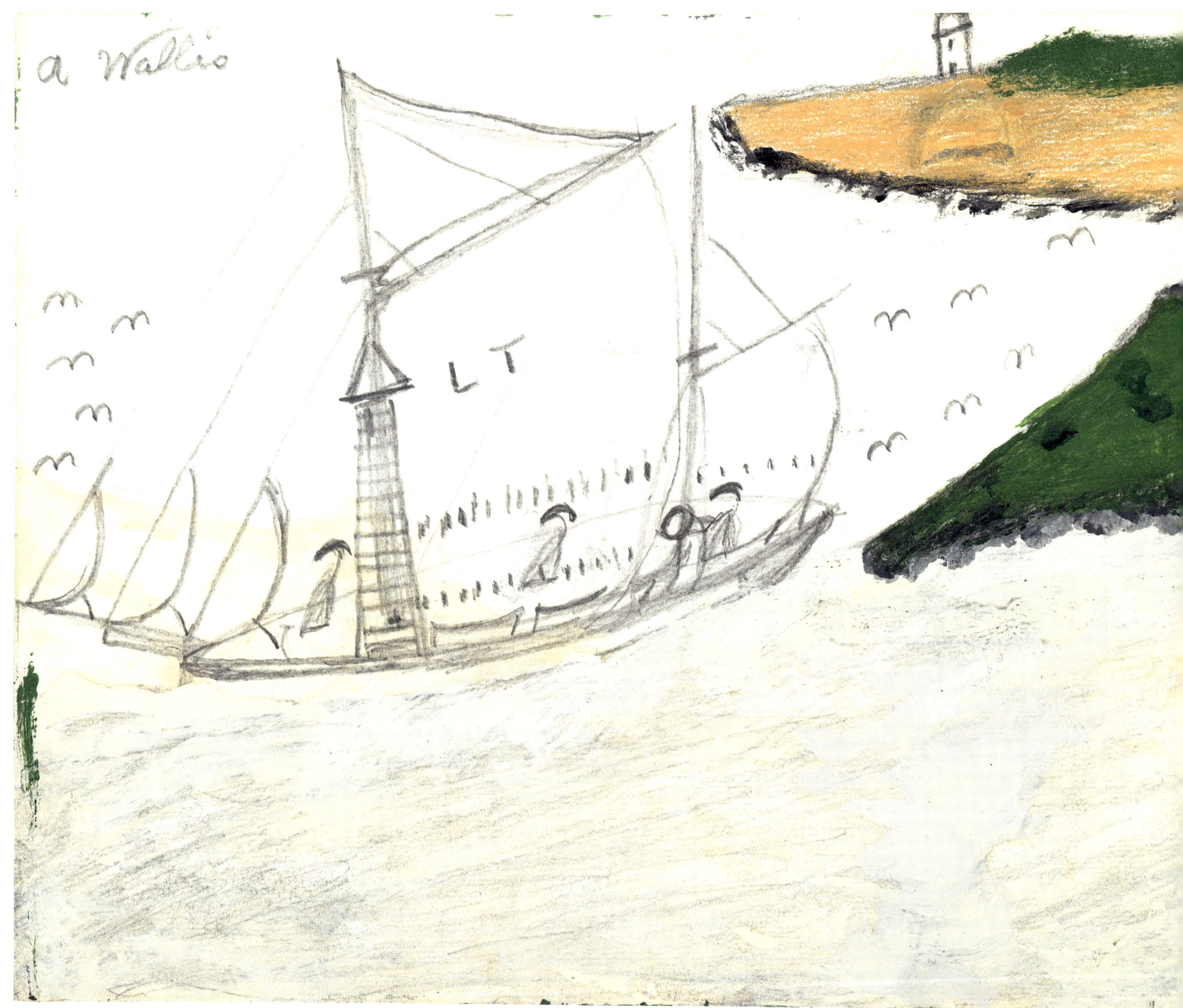

a Wallis
LT

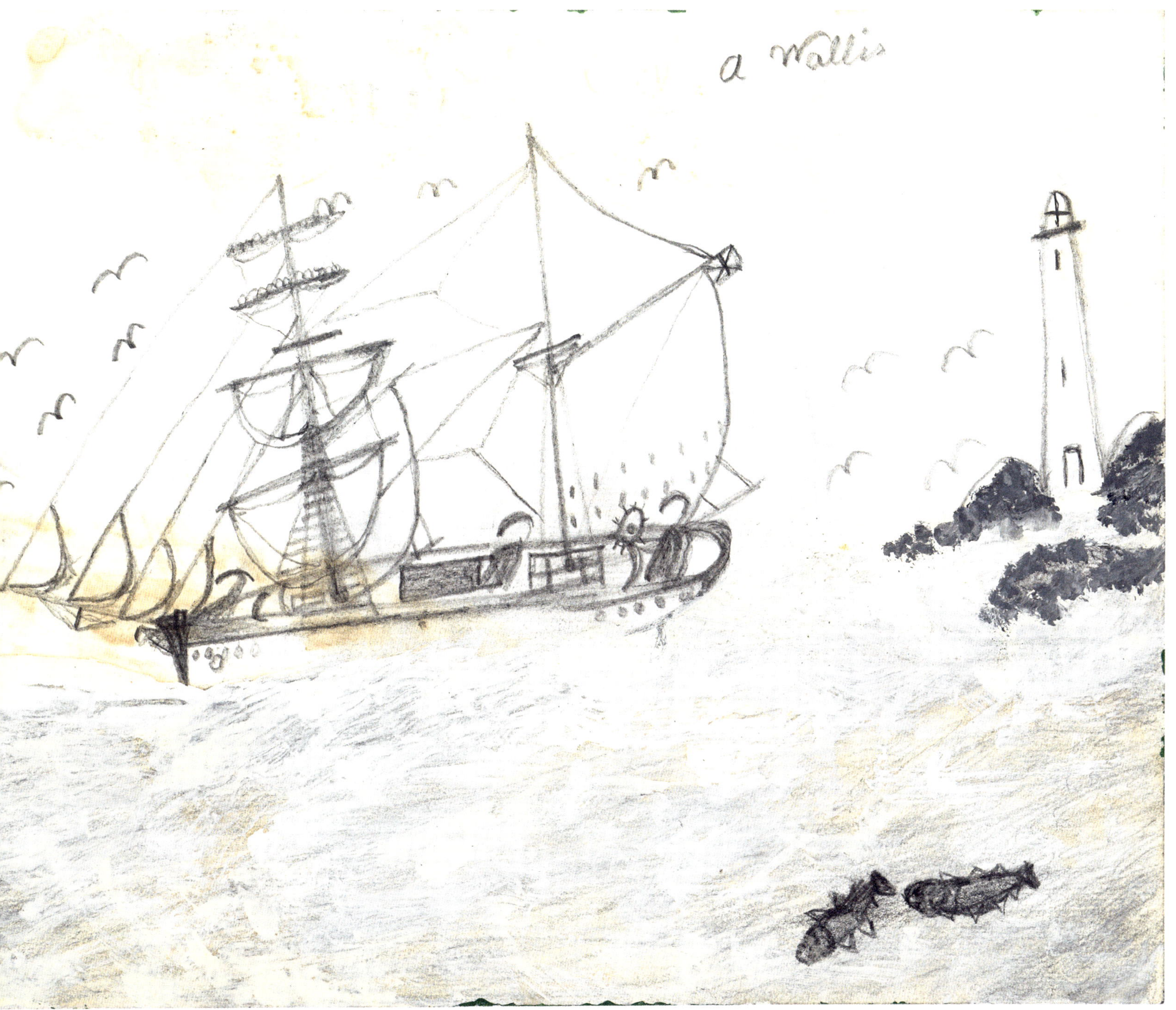
a Wallis

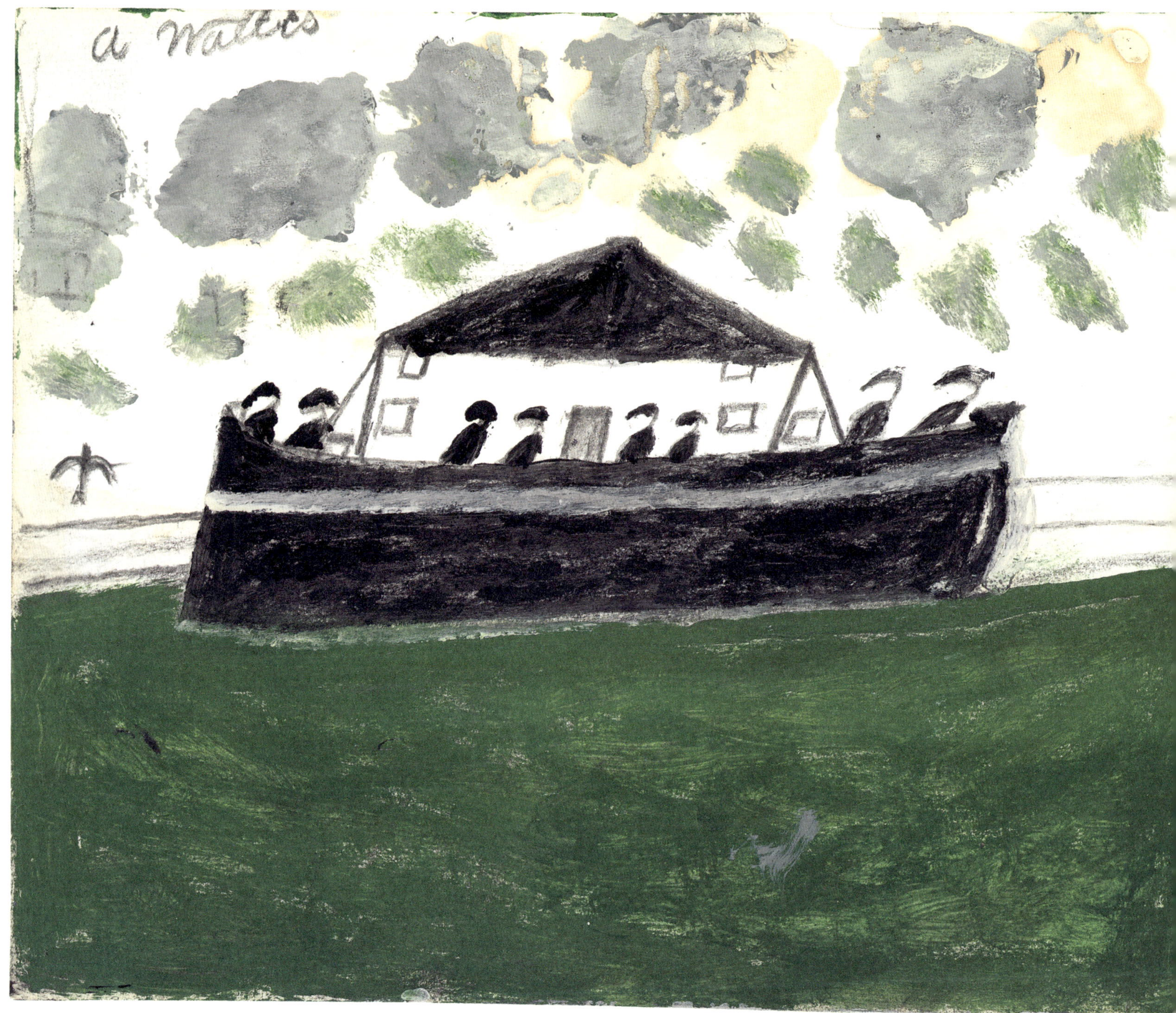
a Wales

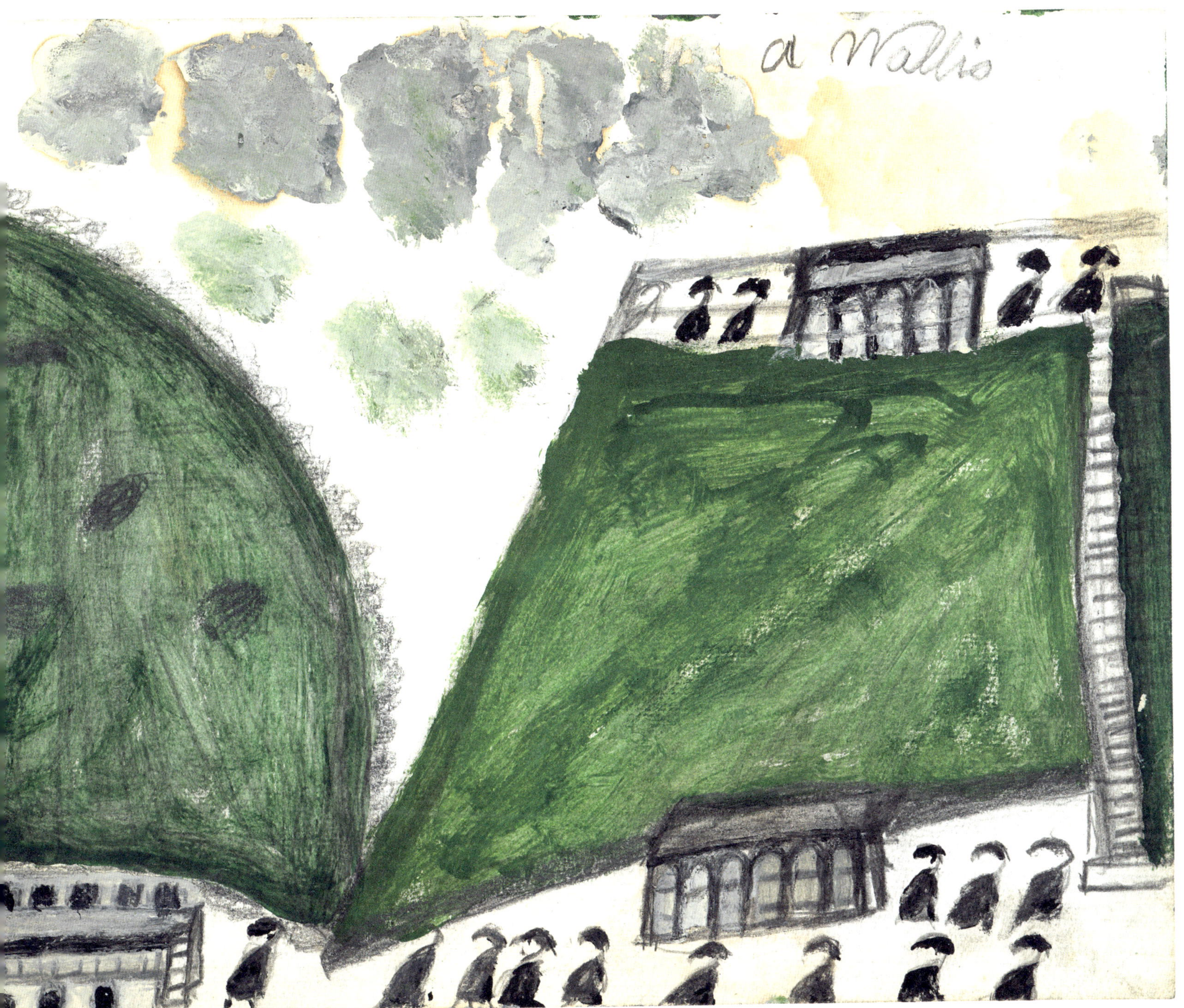
a Wallis

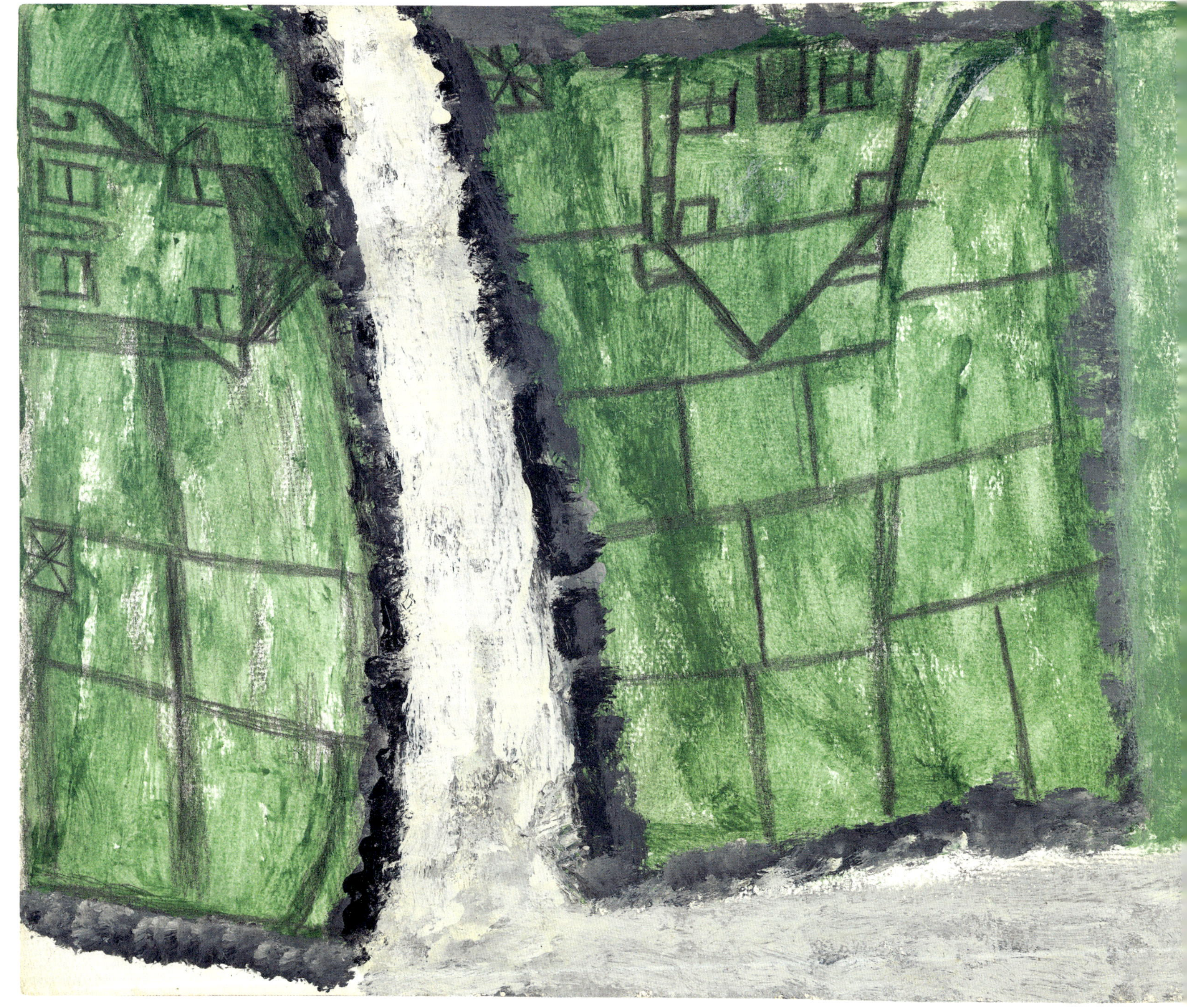

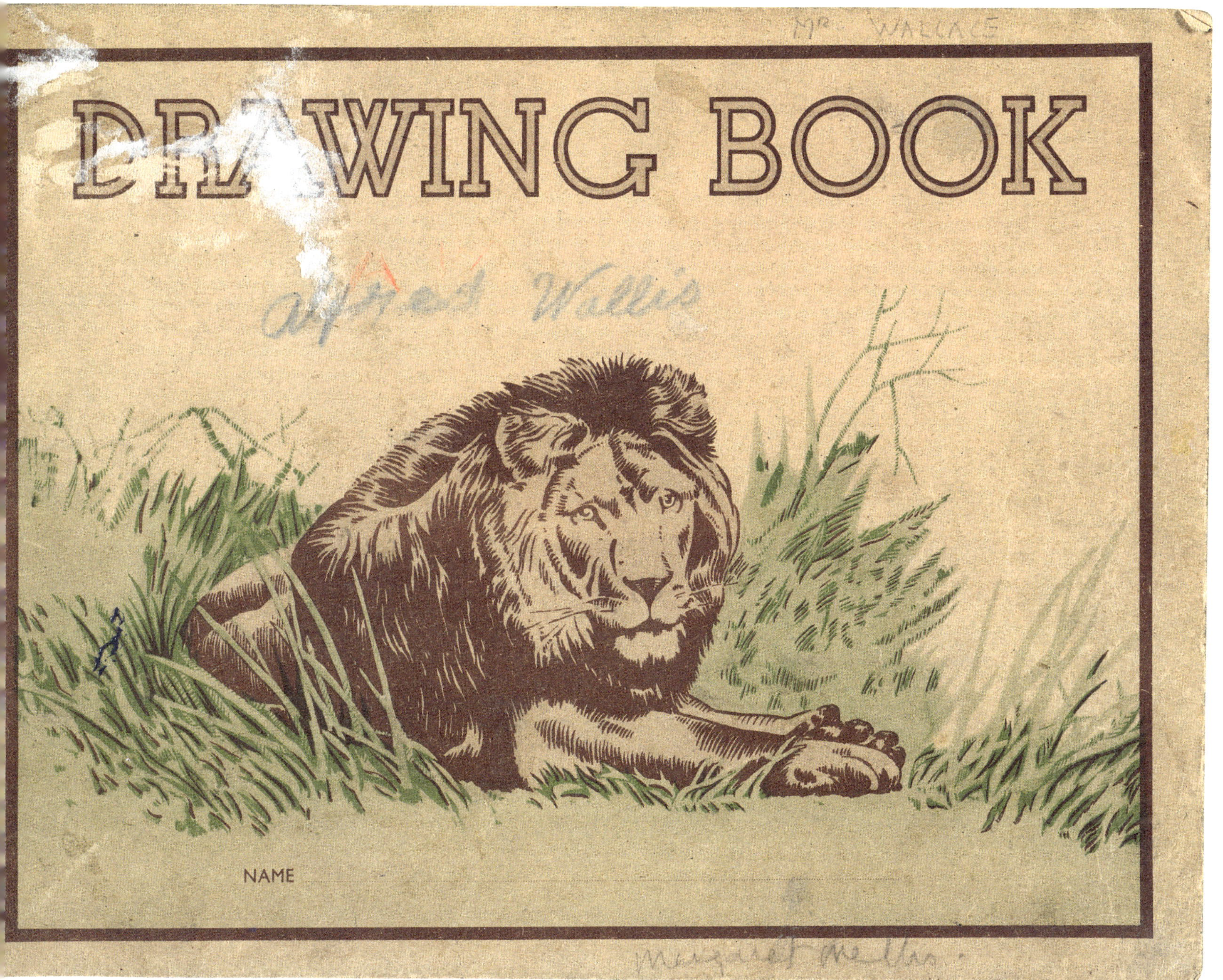

Mr WALLACE
alfred Wallis
DRAWING BOOK
NAME
Margaret Wallis.

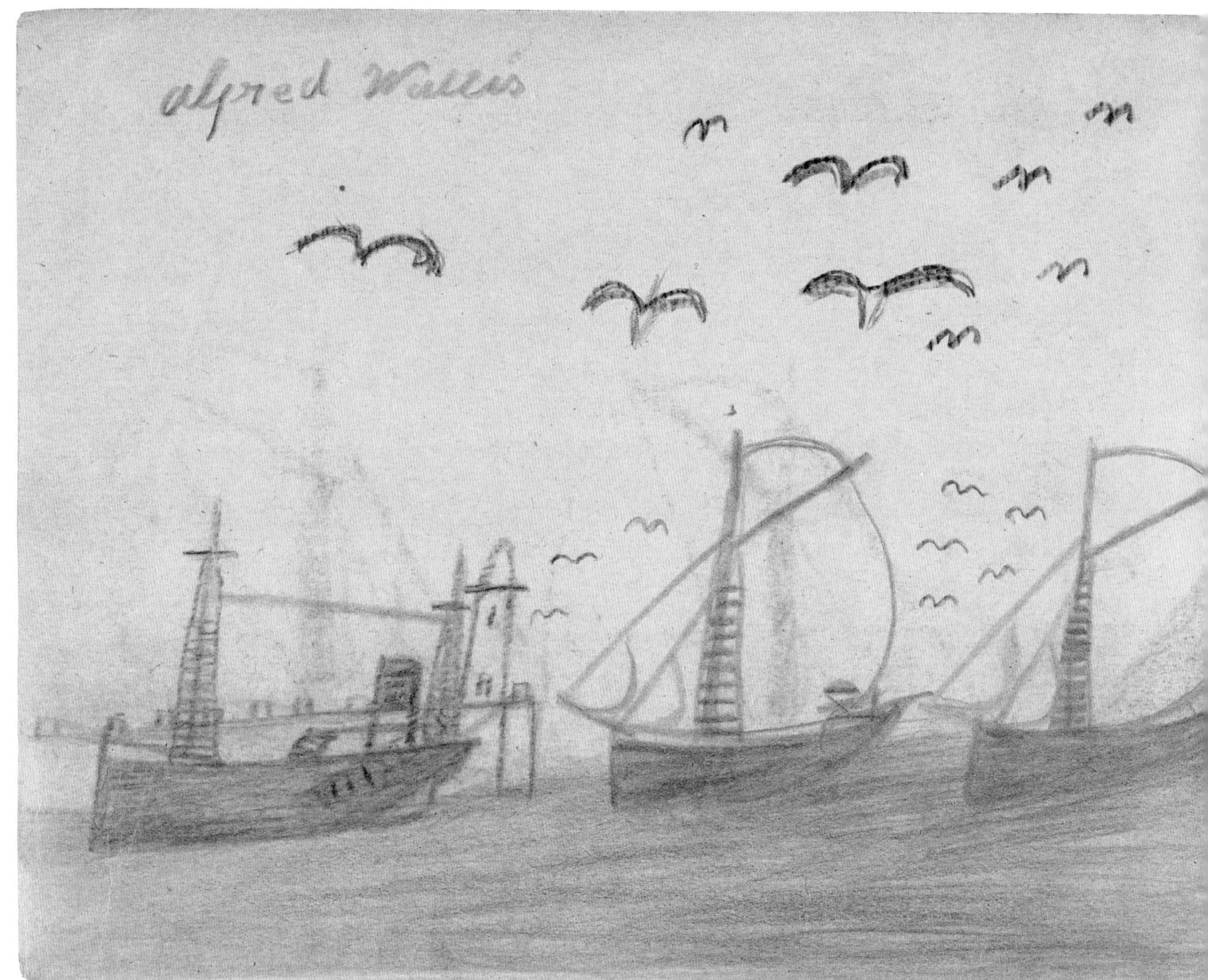

alfred Wallis

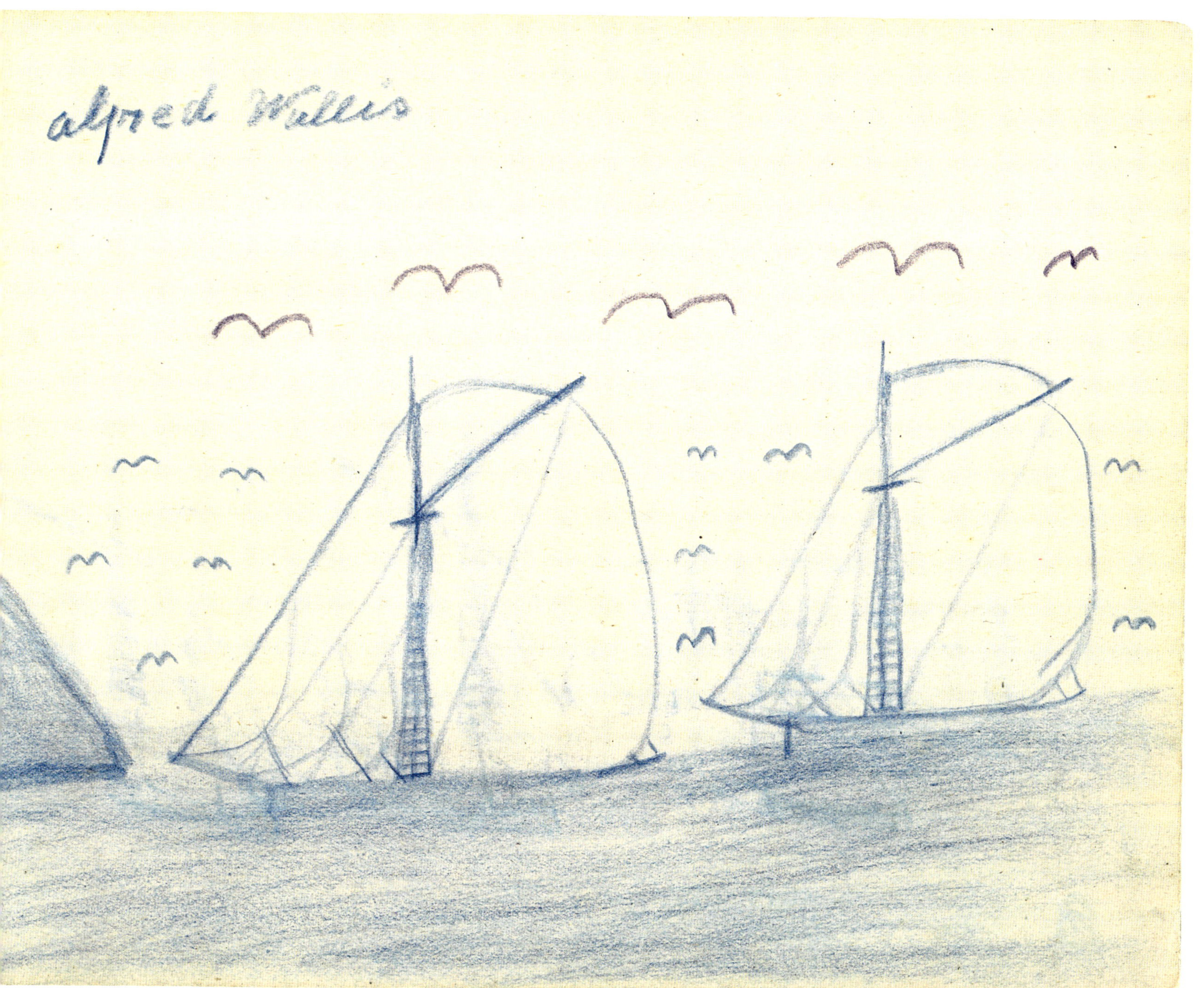

alfred Willis

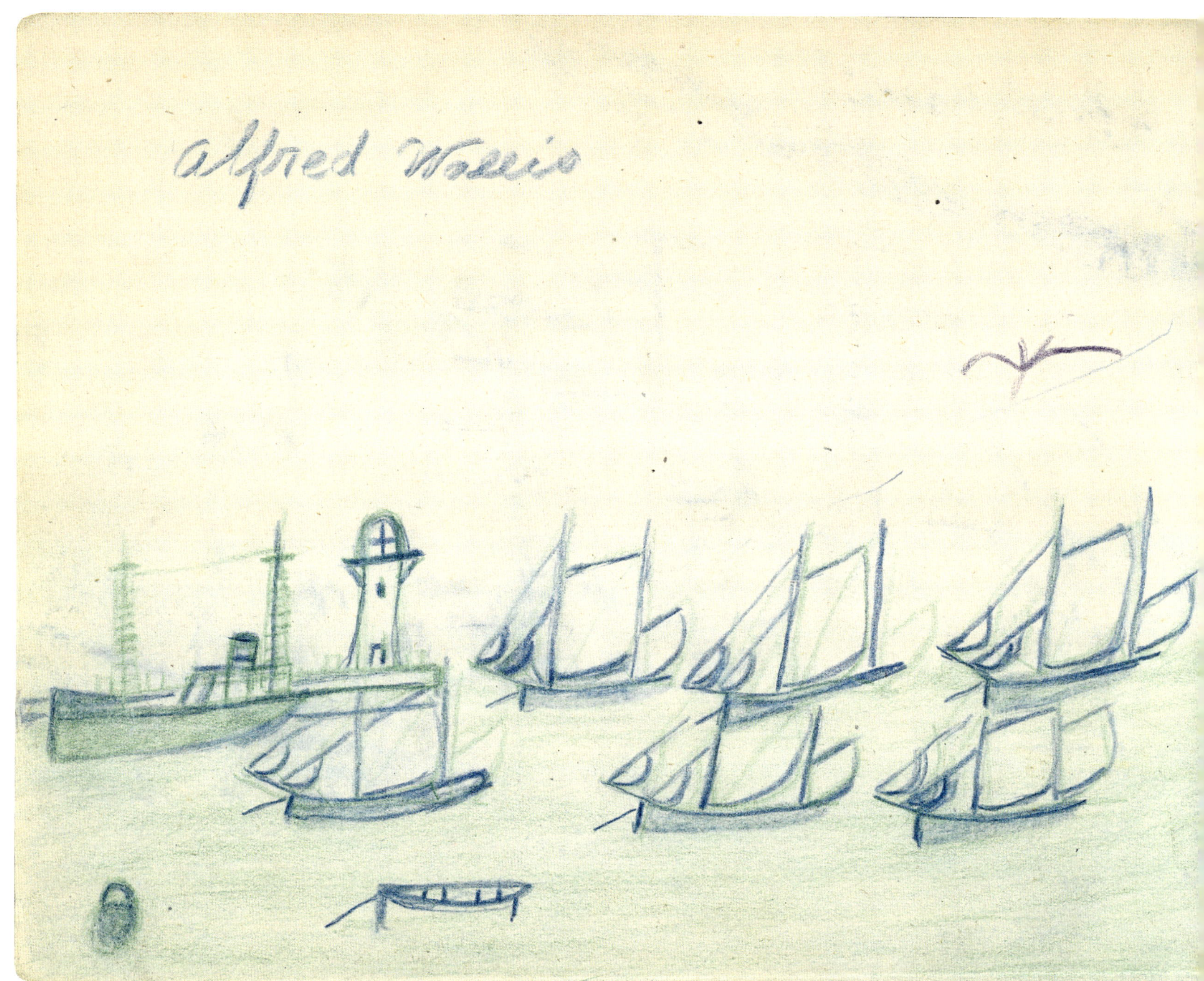
alfred Wallis

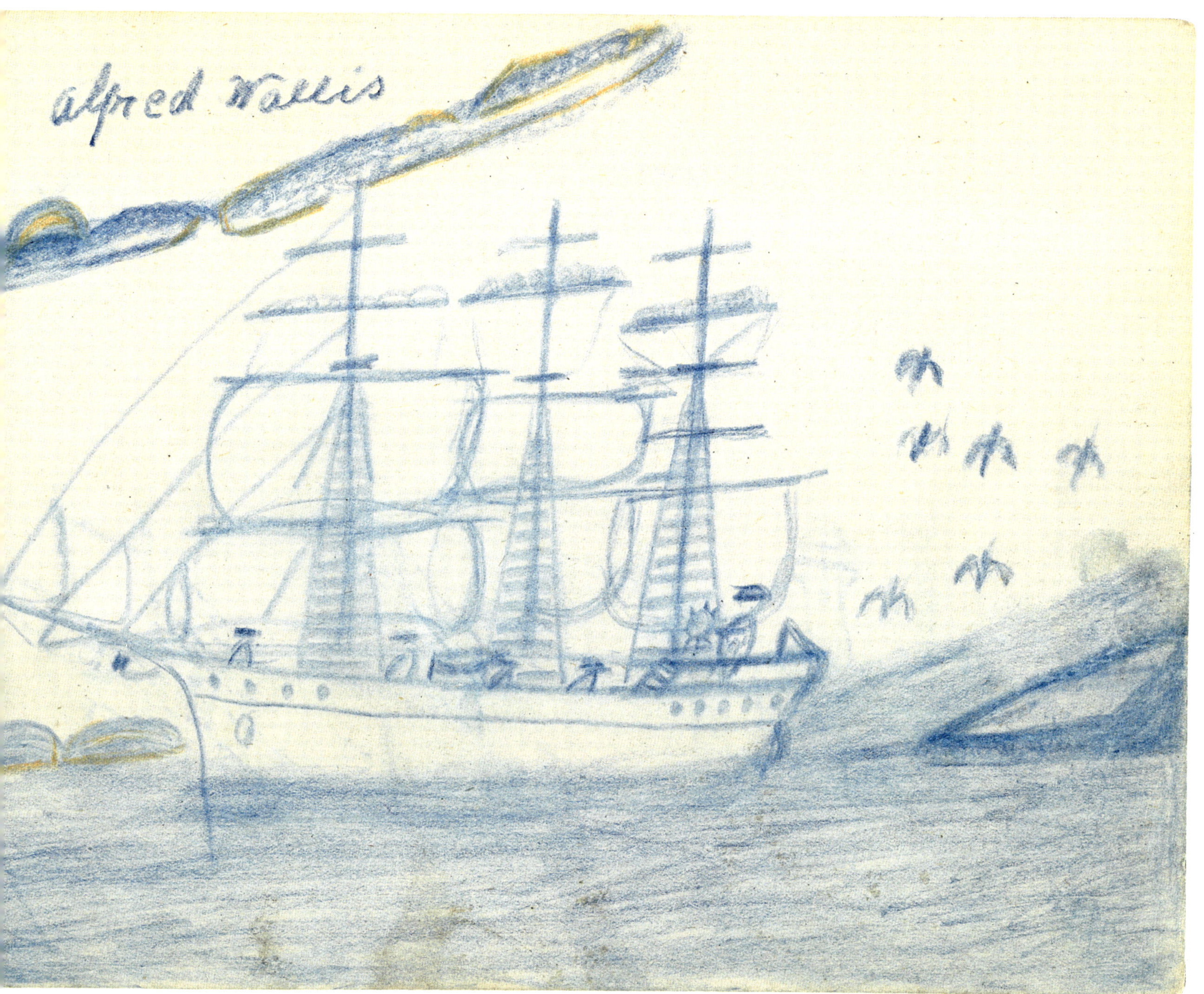

alfred wallis

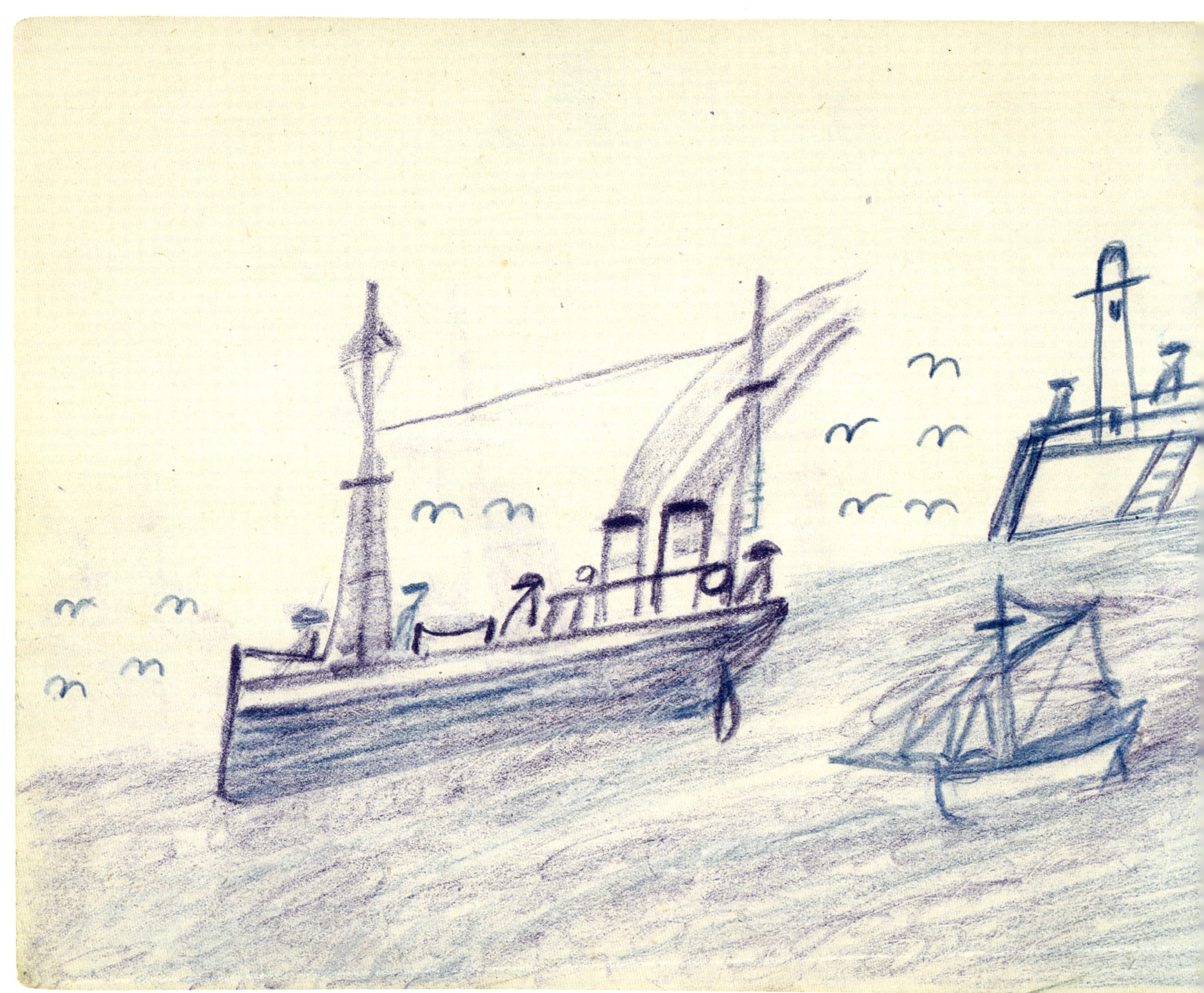

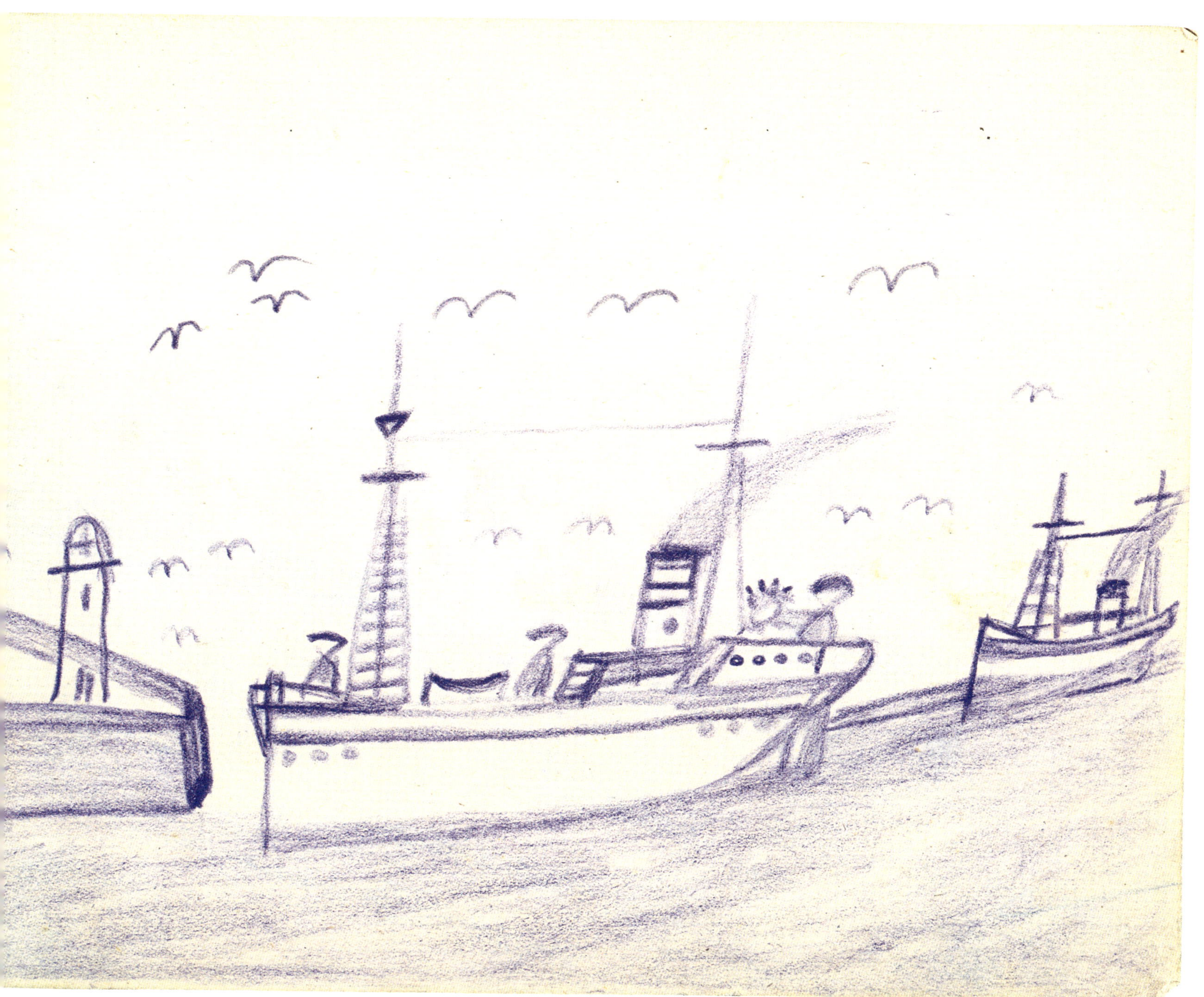

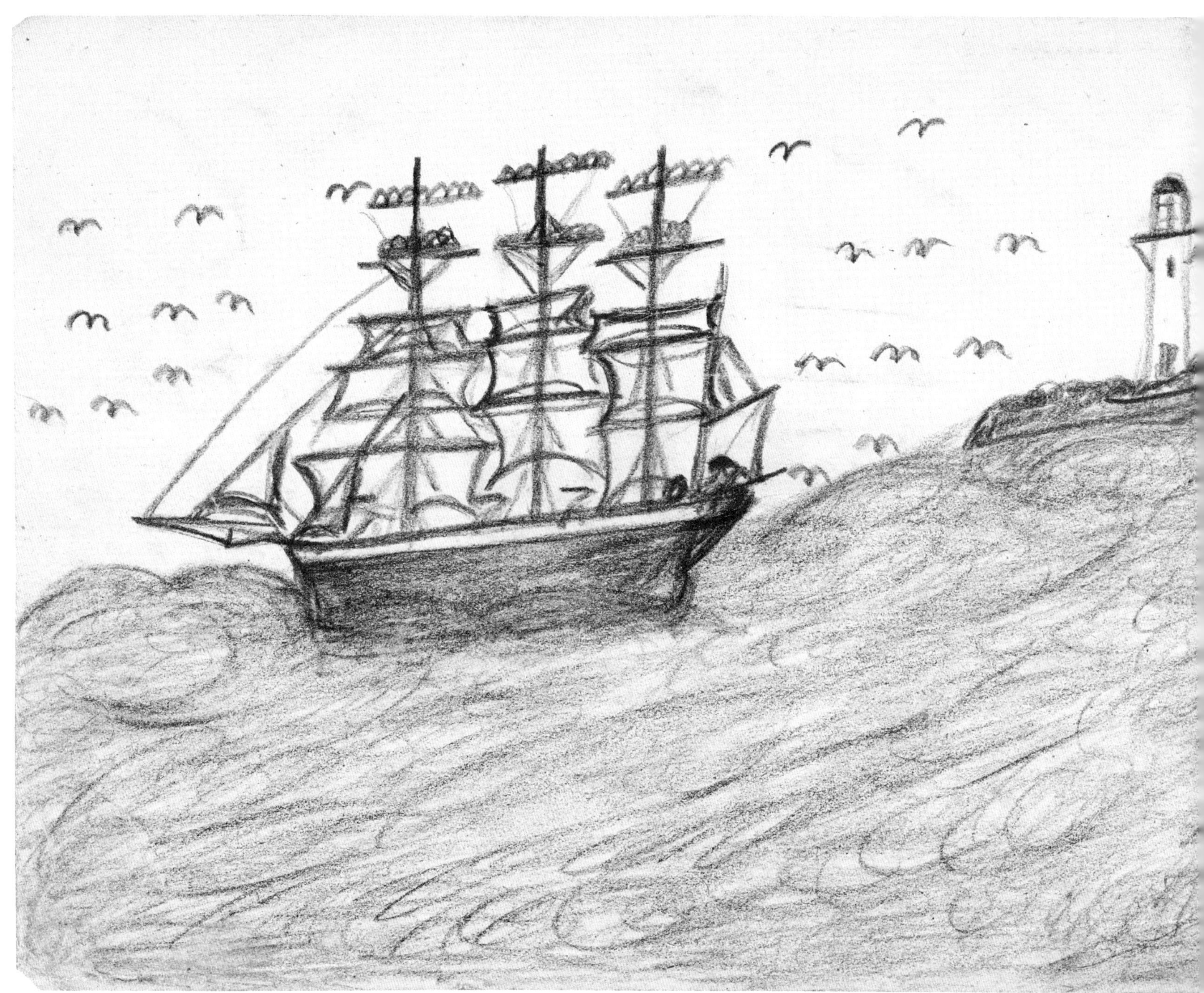

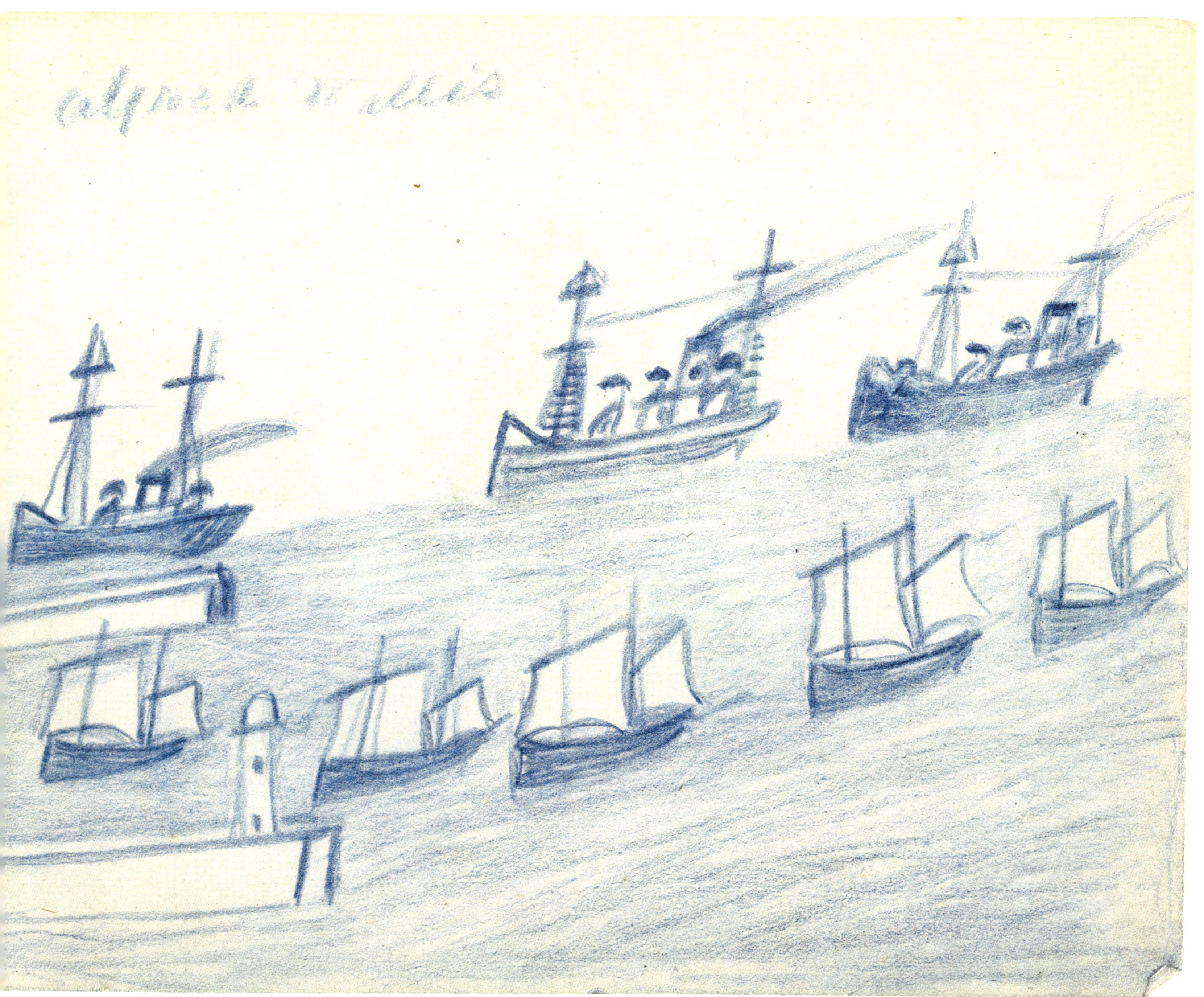
alfred wallis

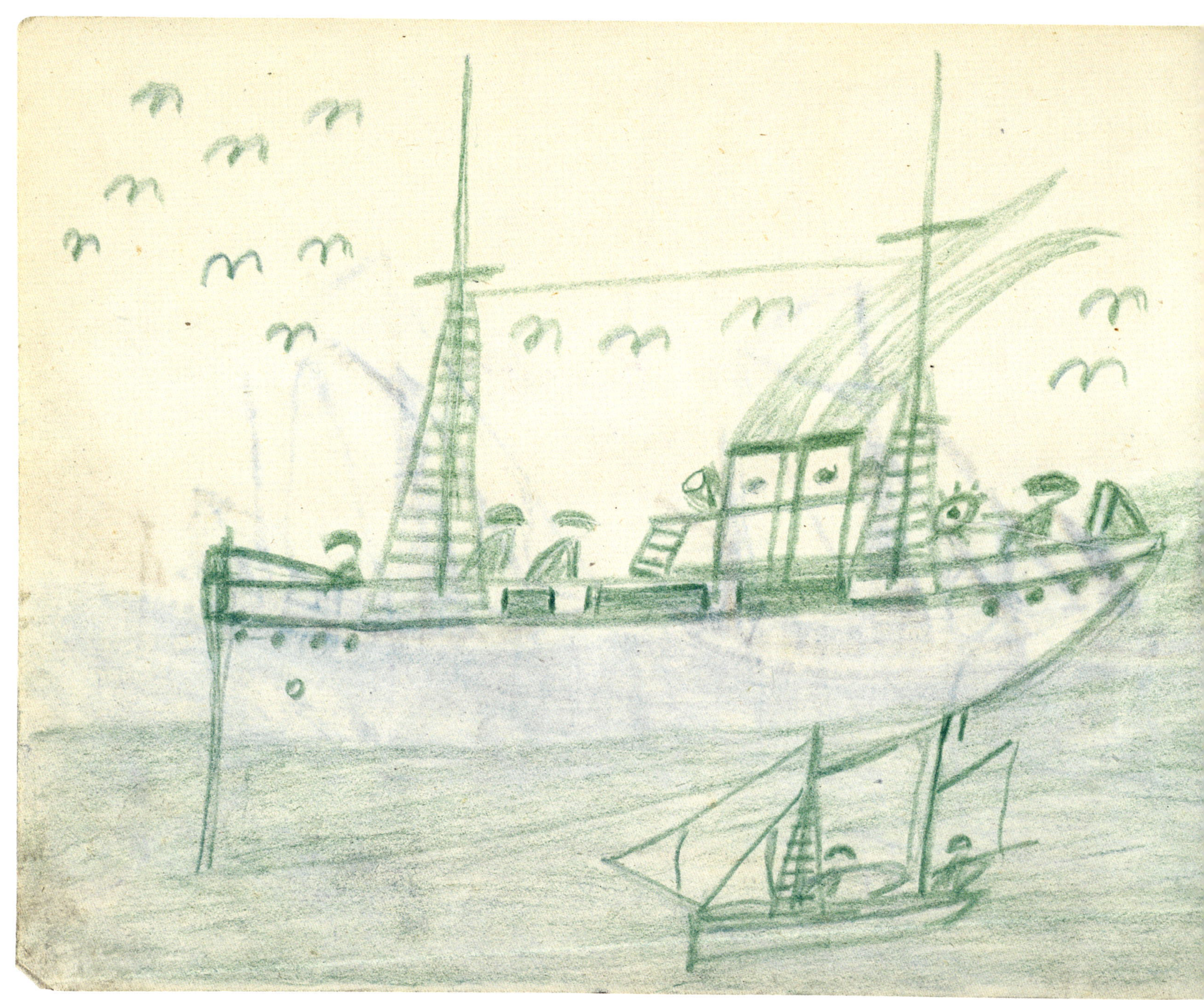

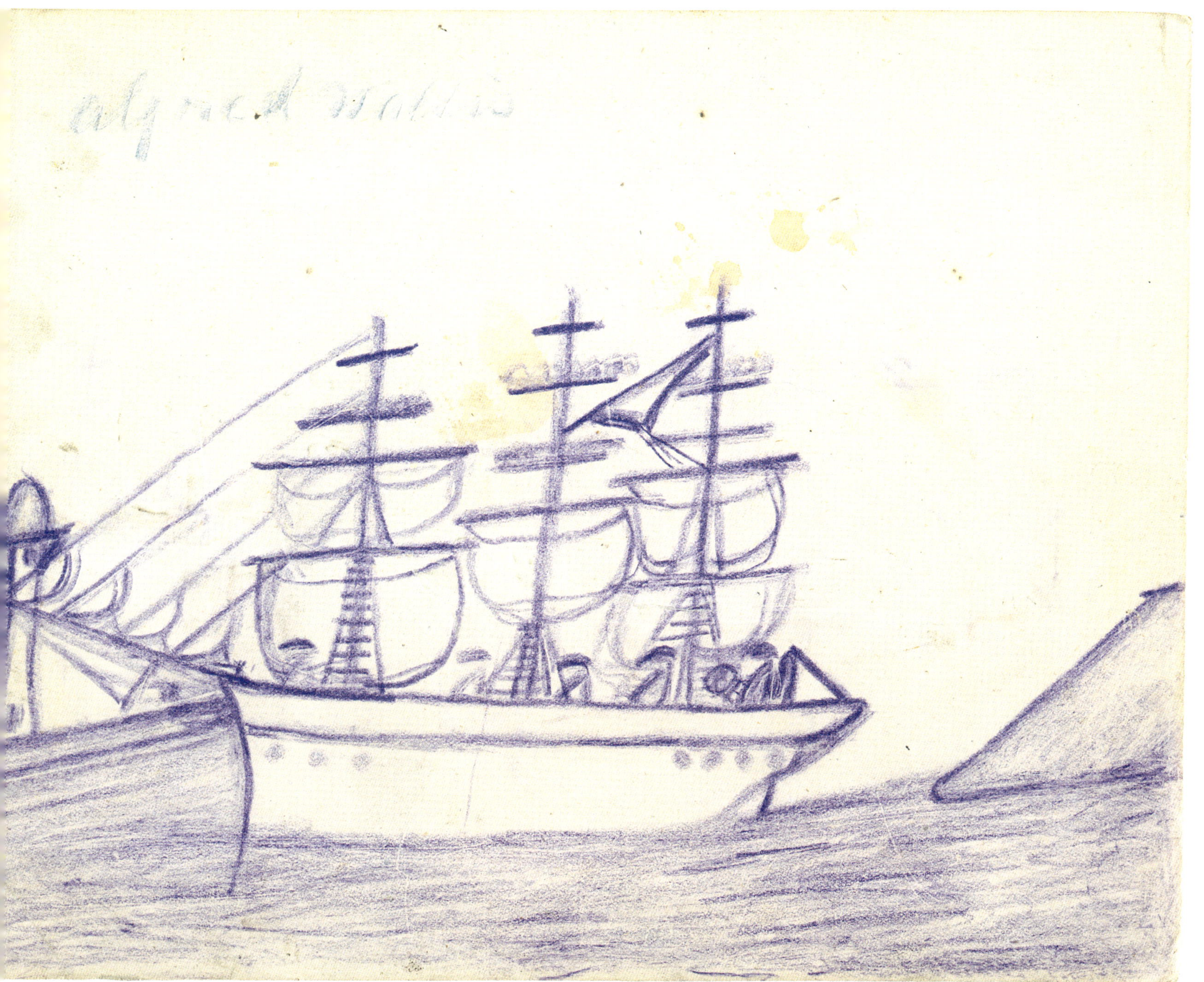

alfred wallis

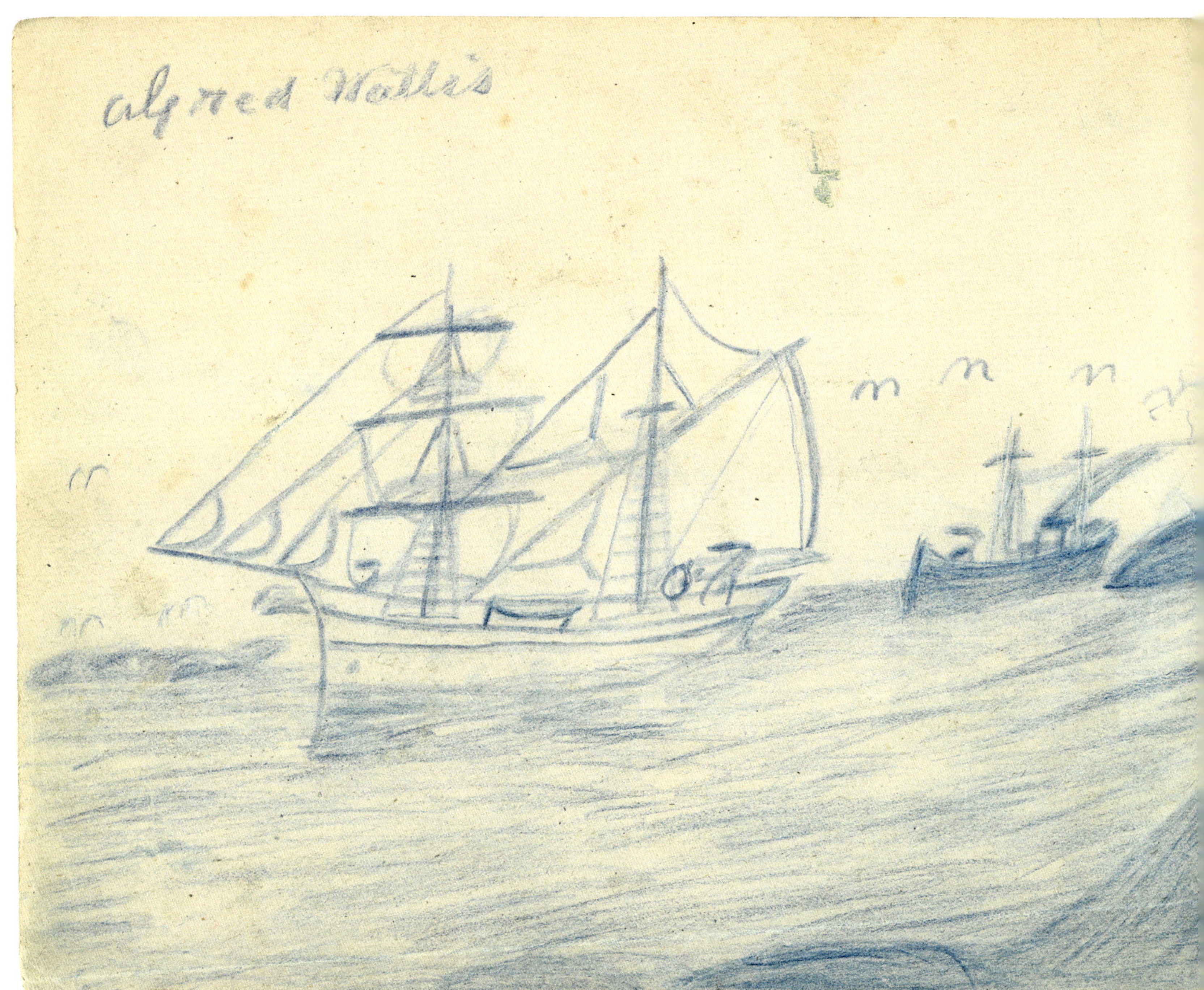

Alfred Wallis

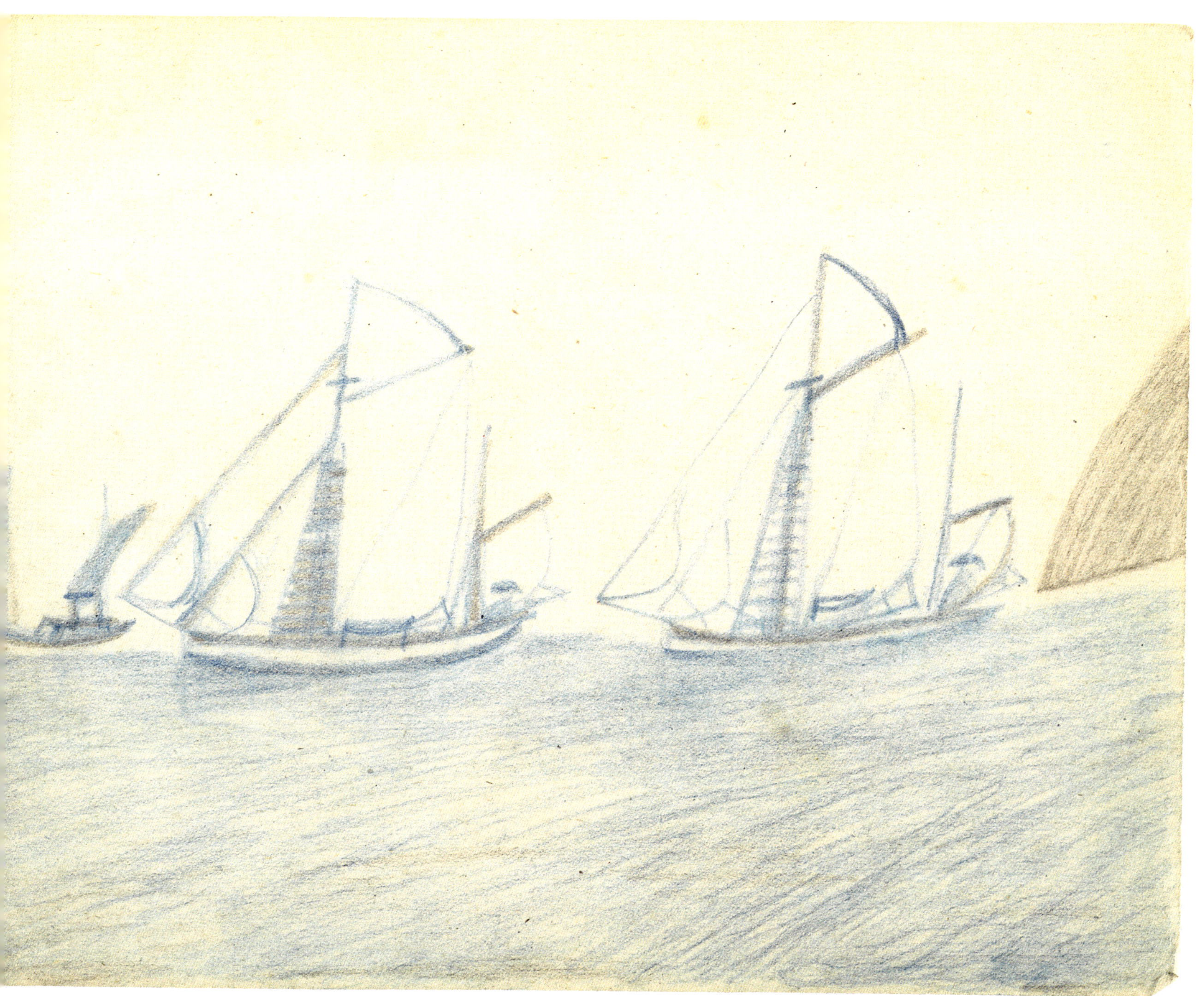

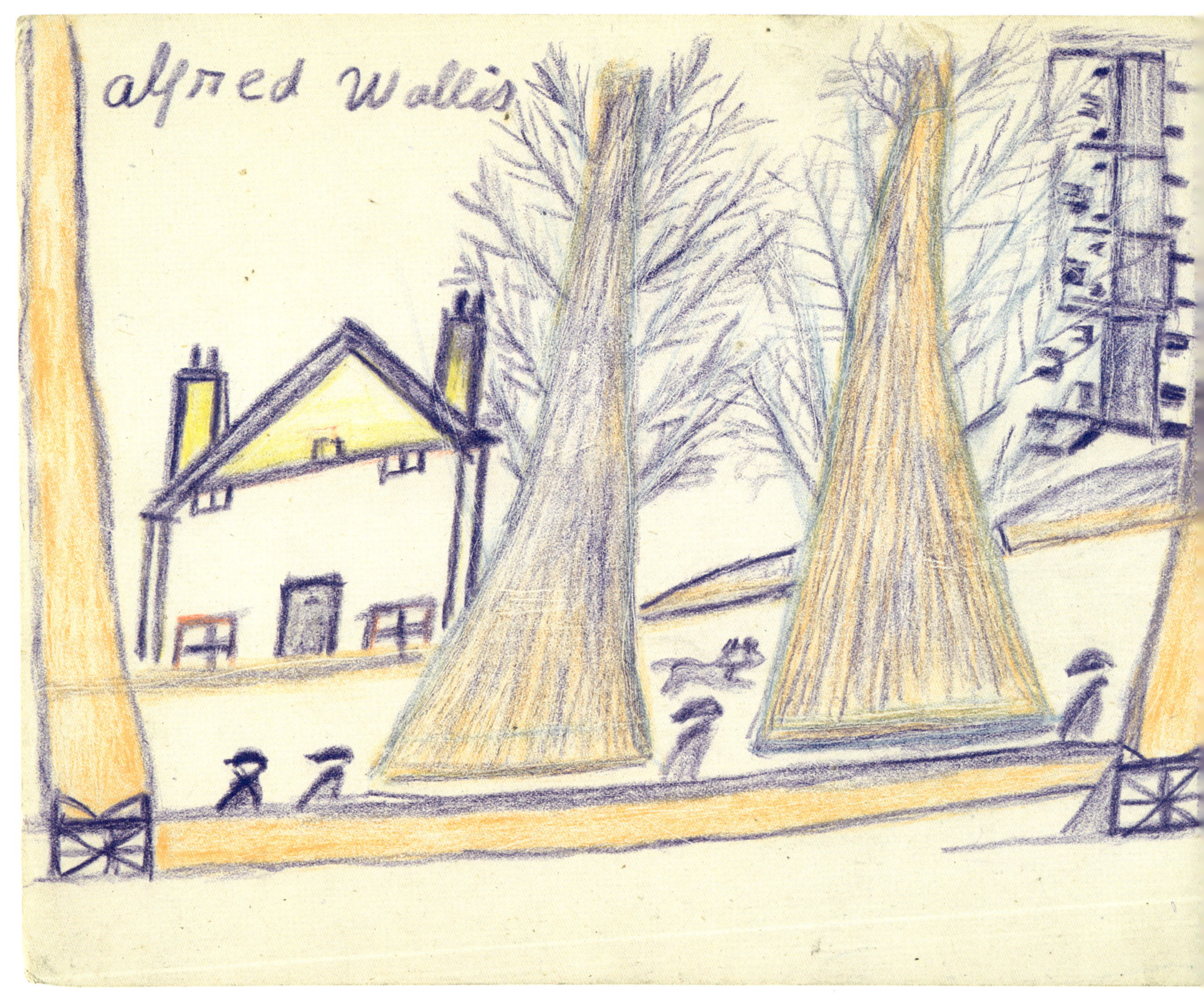
alfred Wallis

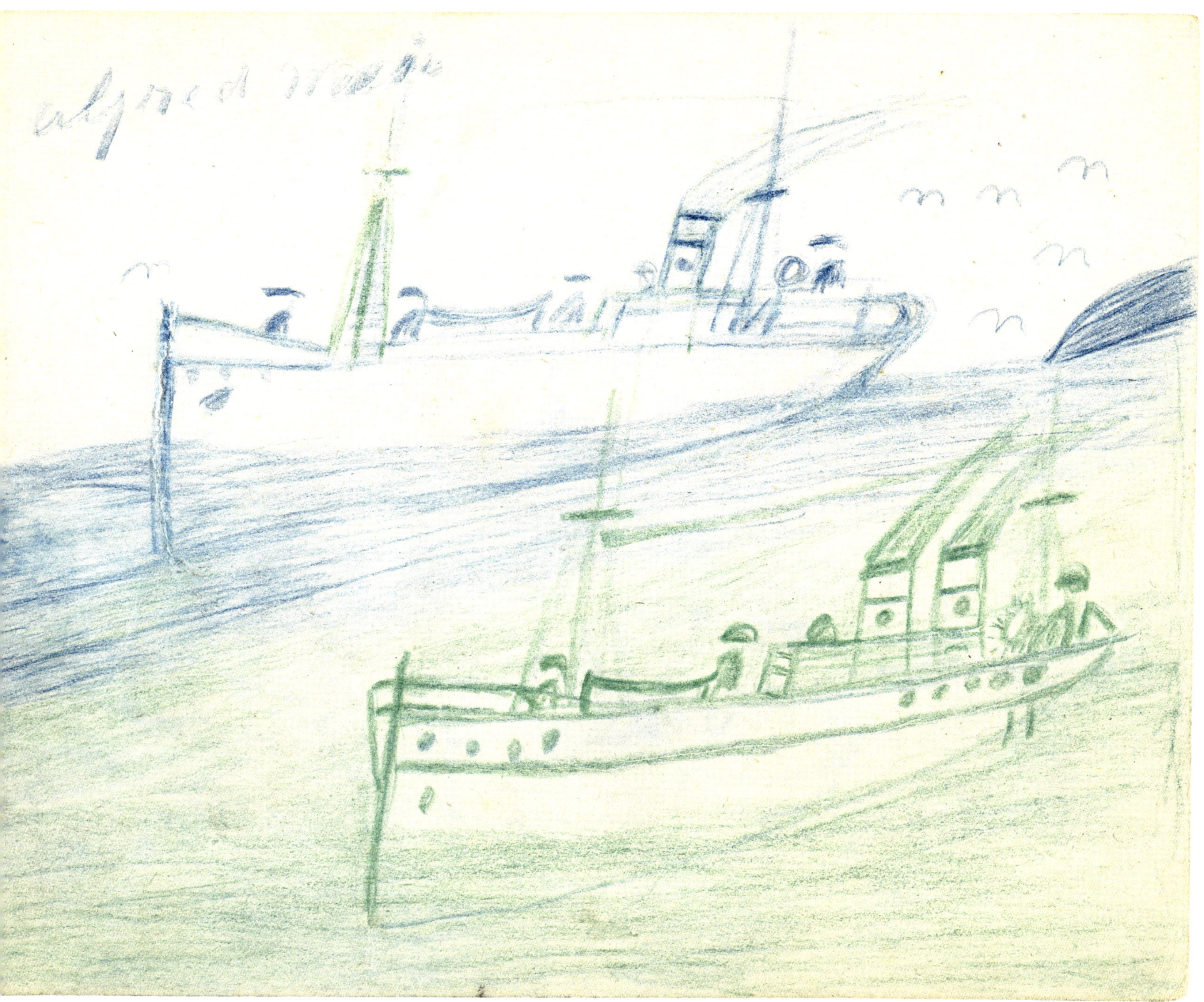

alfred wallis

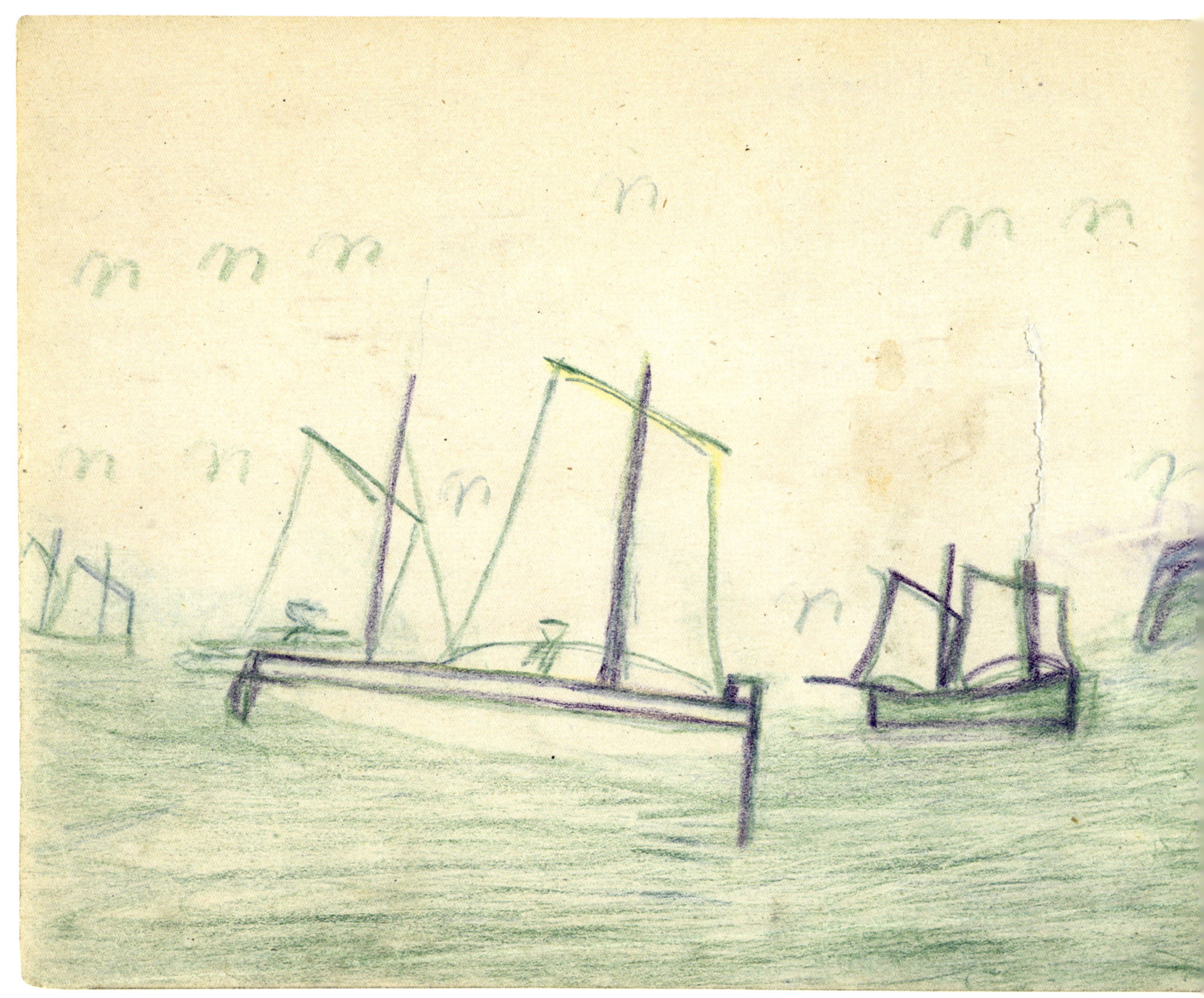

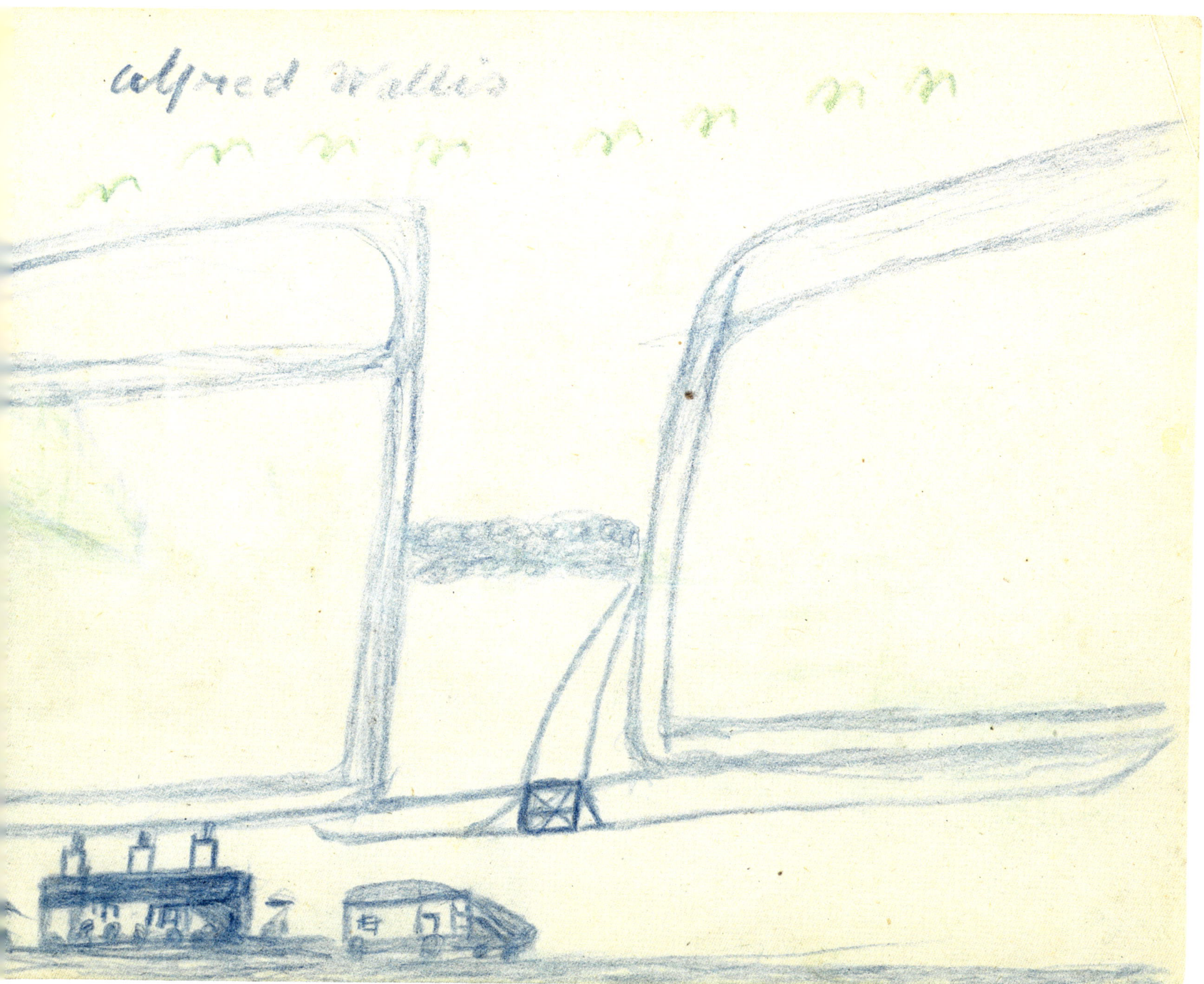
alfred wallis

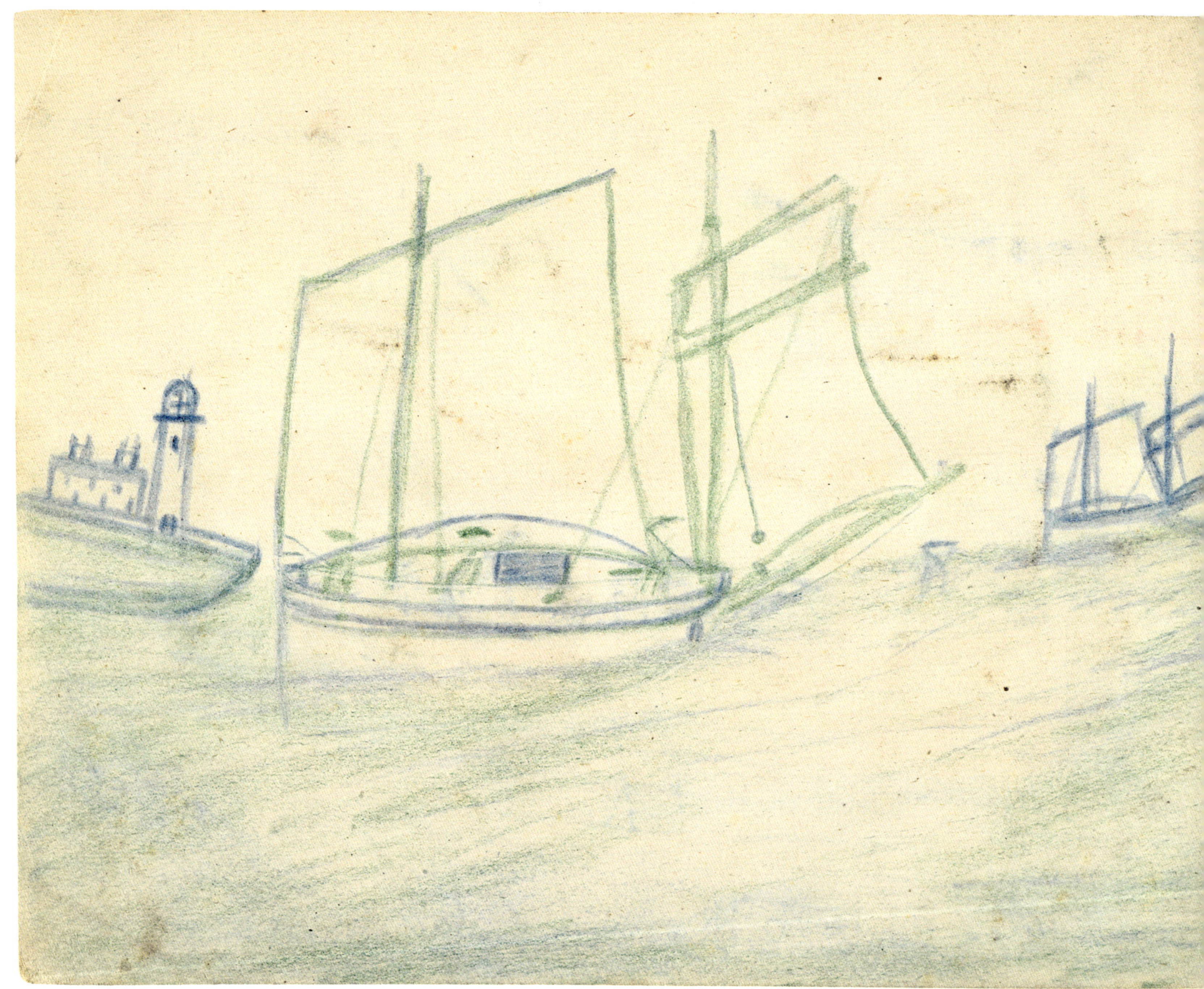

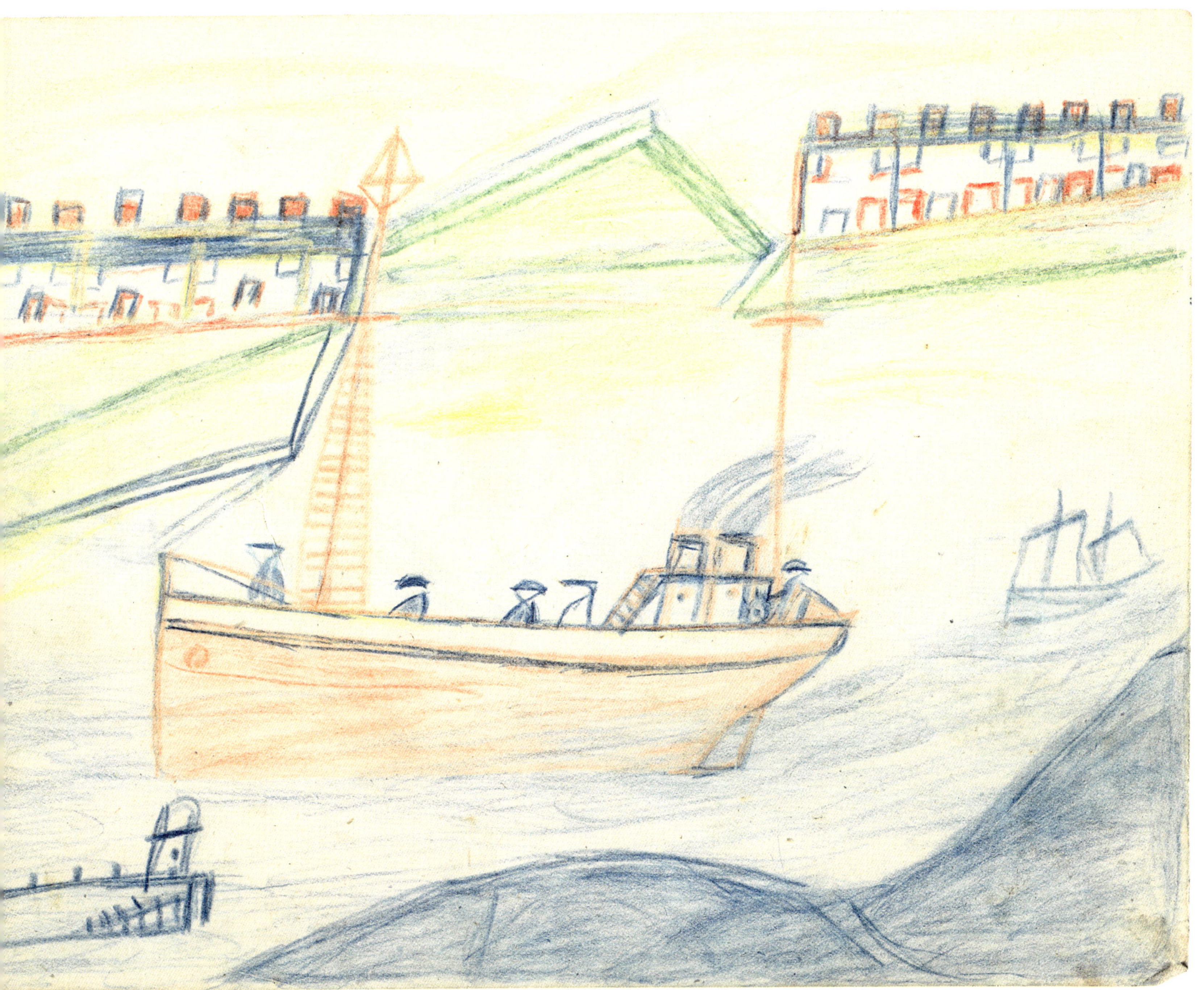

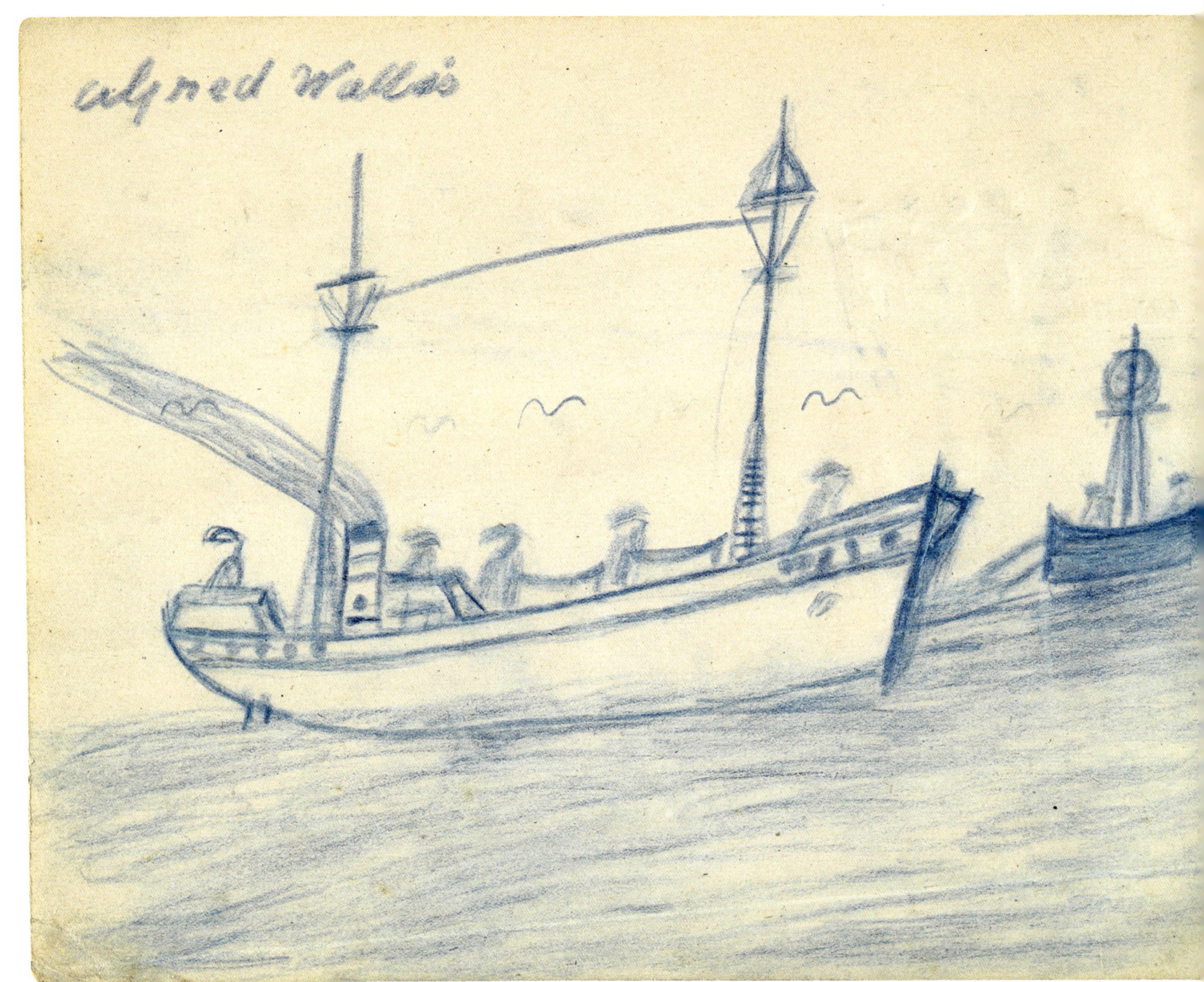
alfred wallis

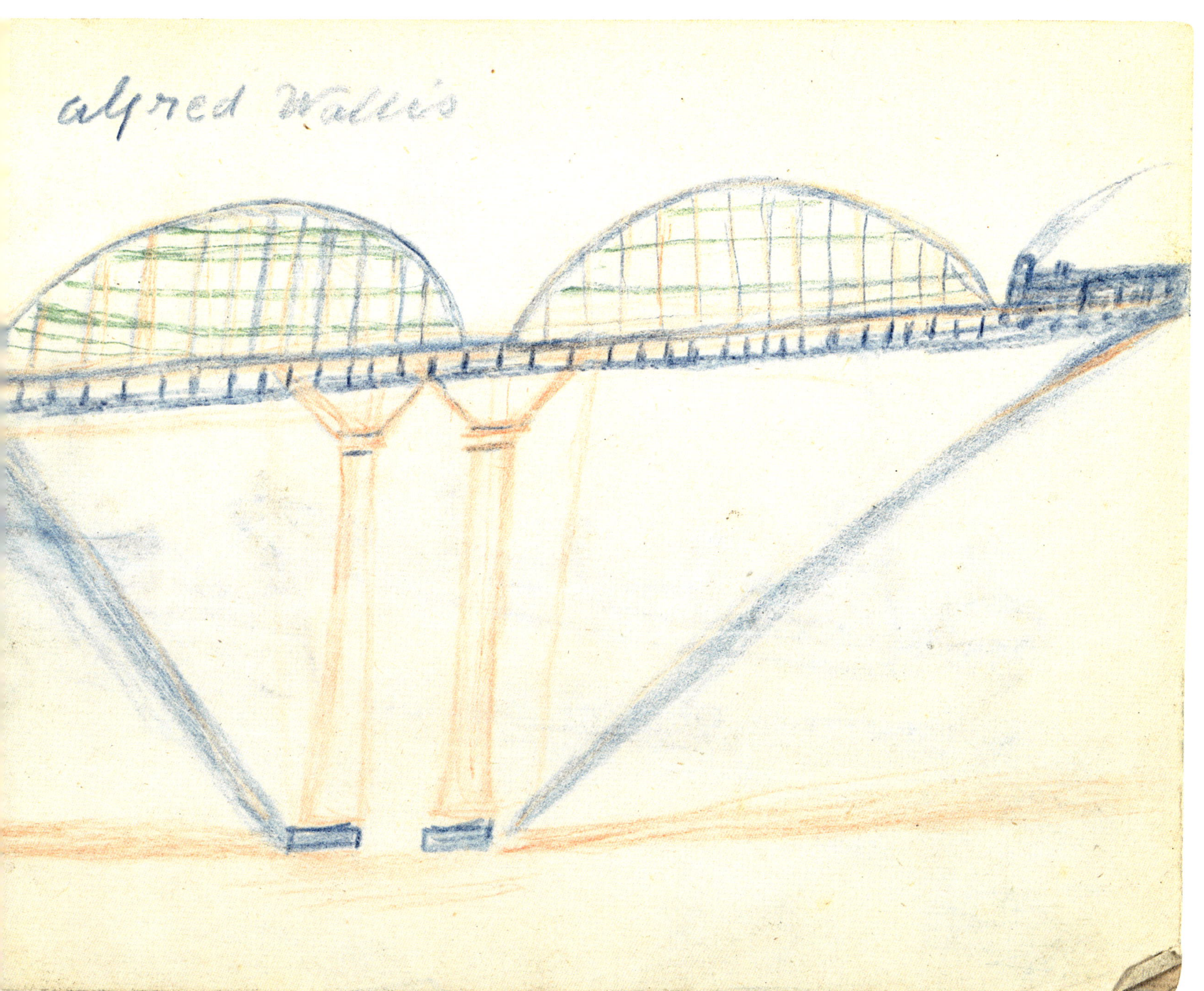

alfred wallis

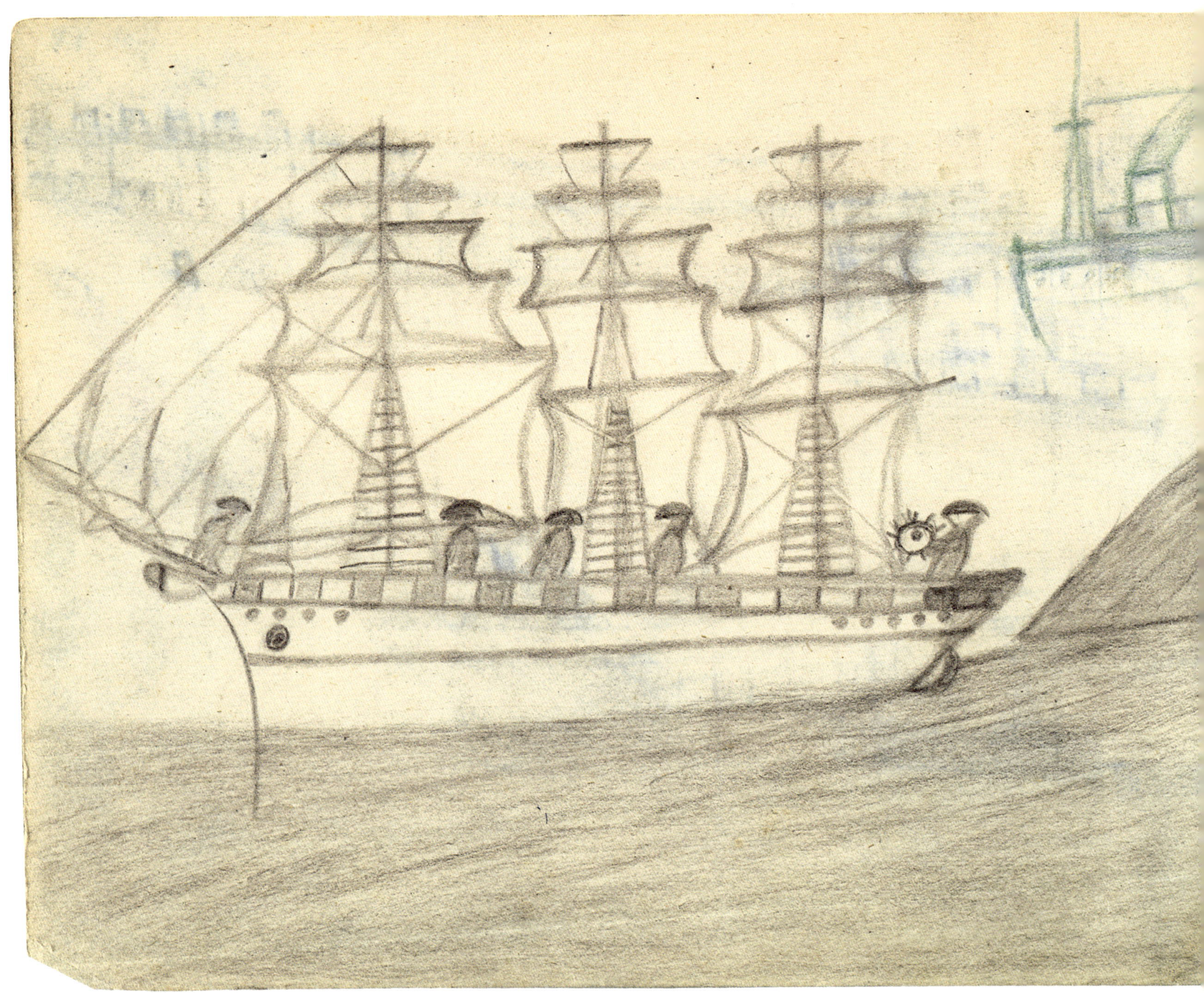

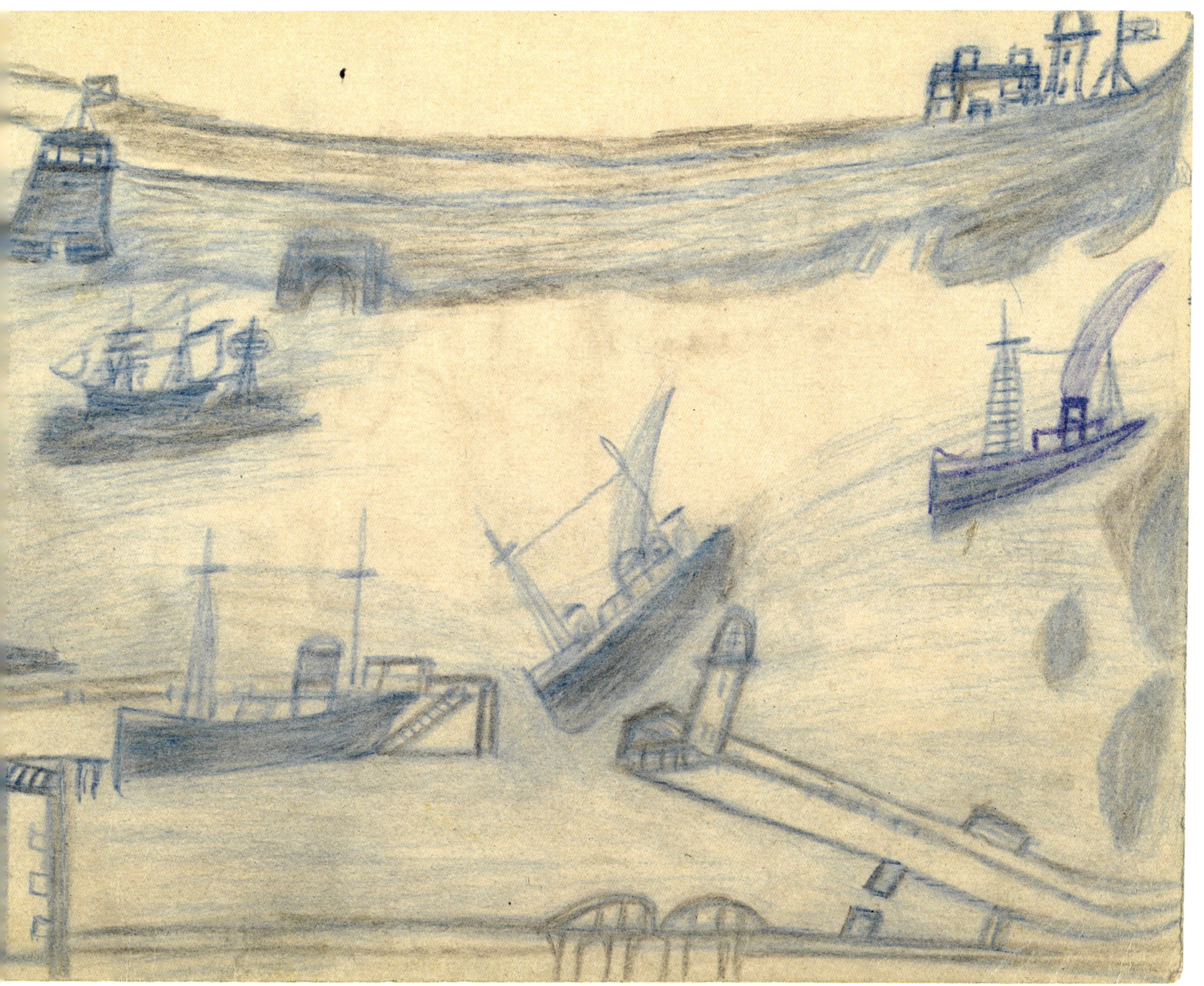

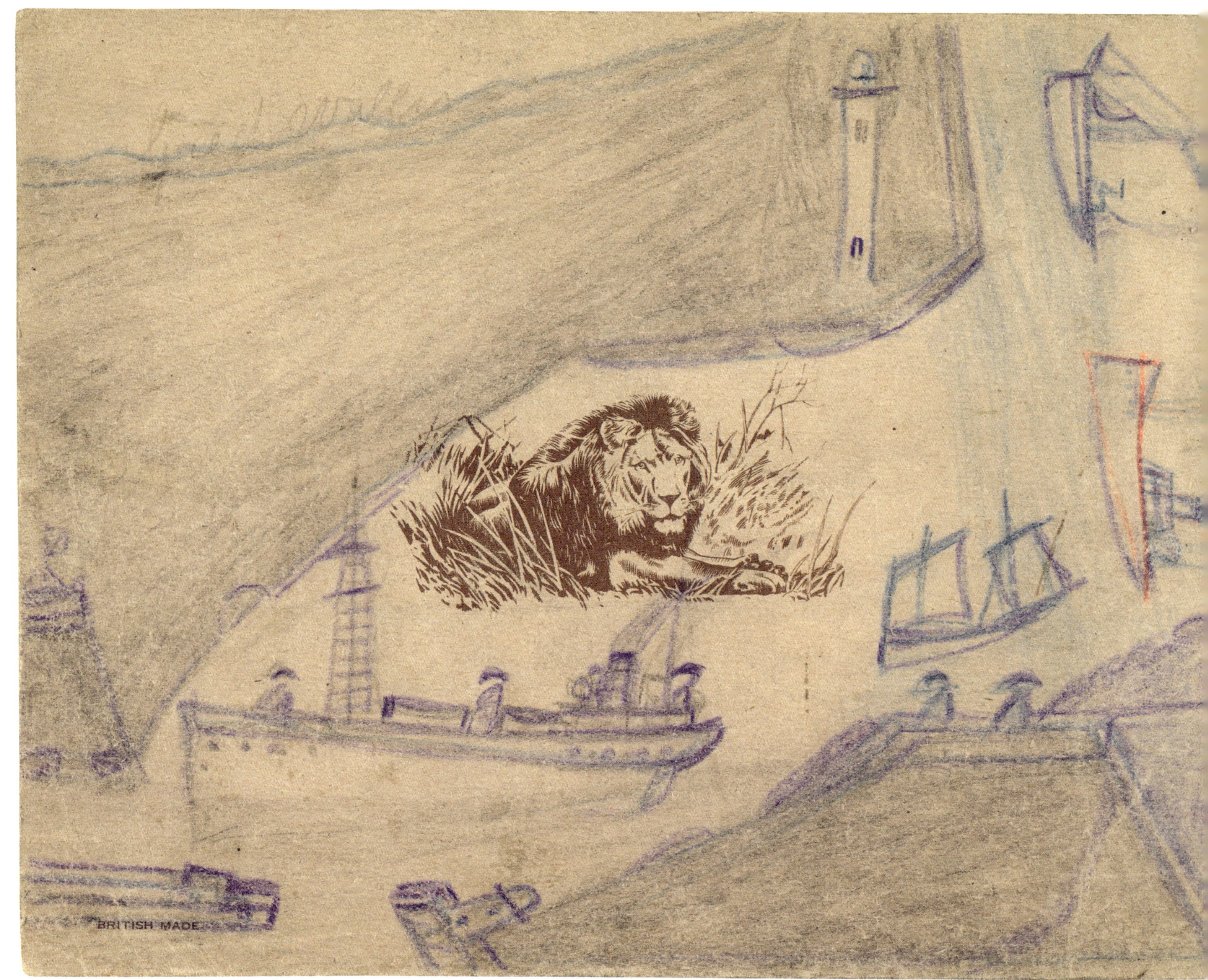

BRITISH MADE

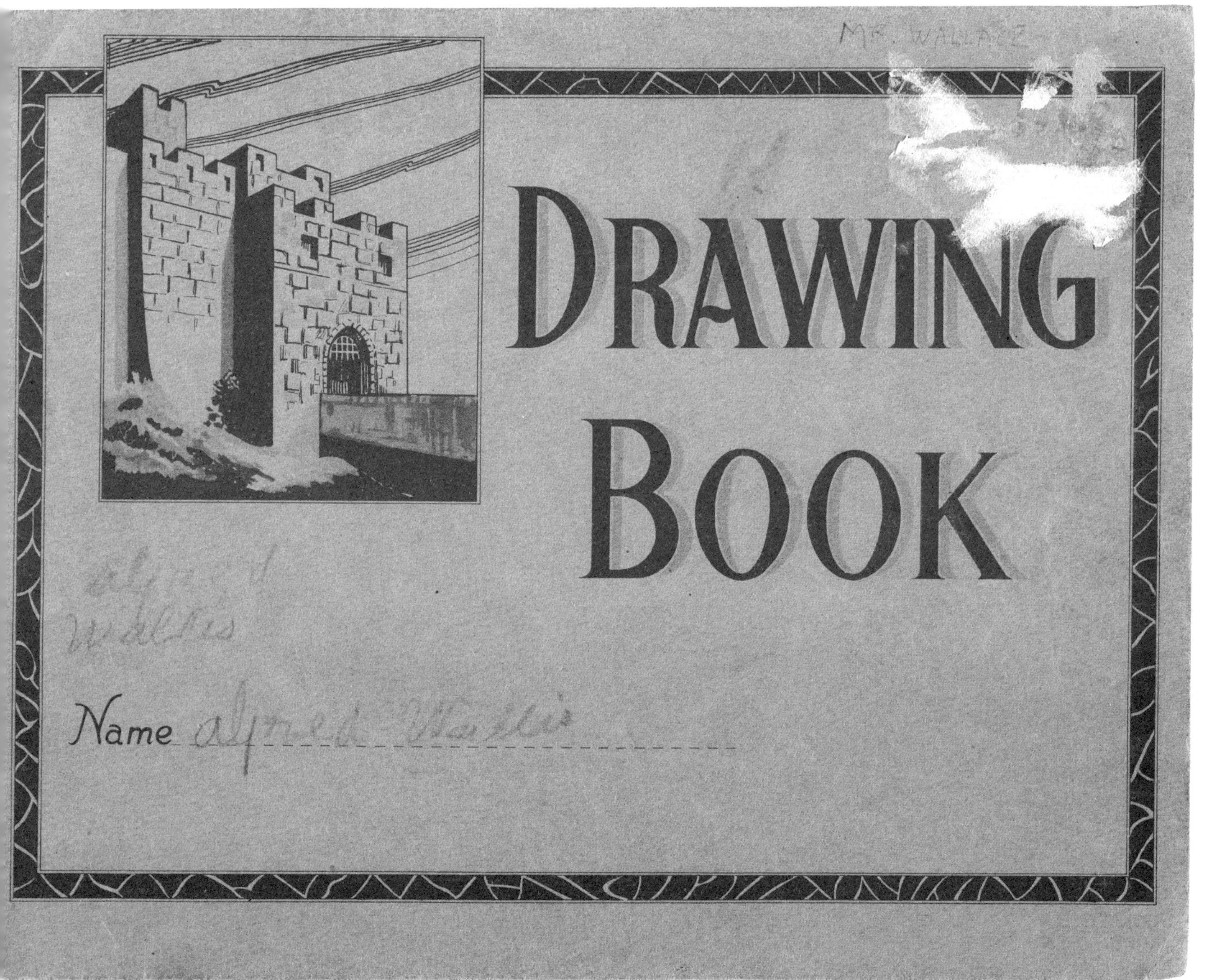
MR. WALLACE
DRAWING
BOOK
alfred
wallis
Name alfred Wallis

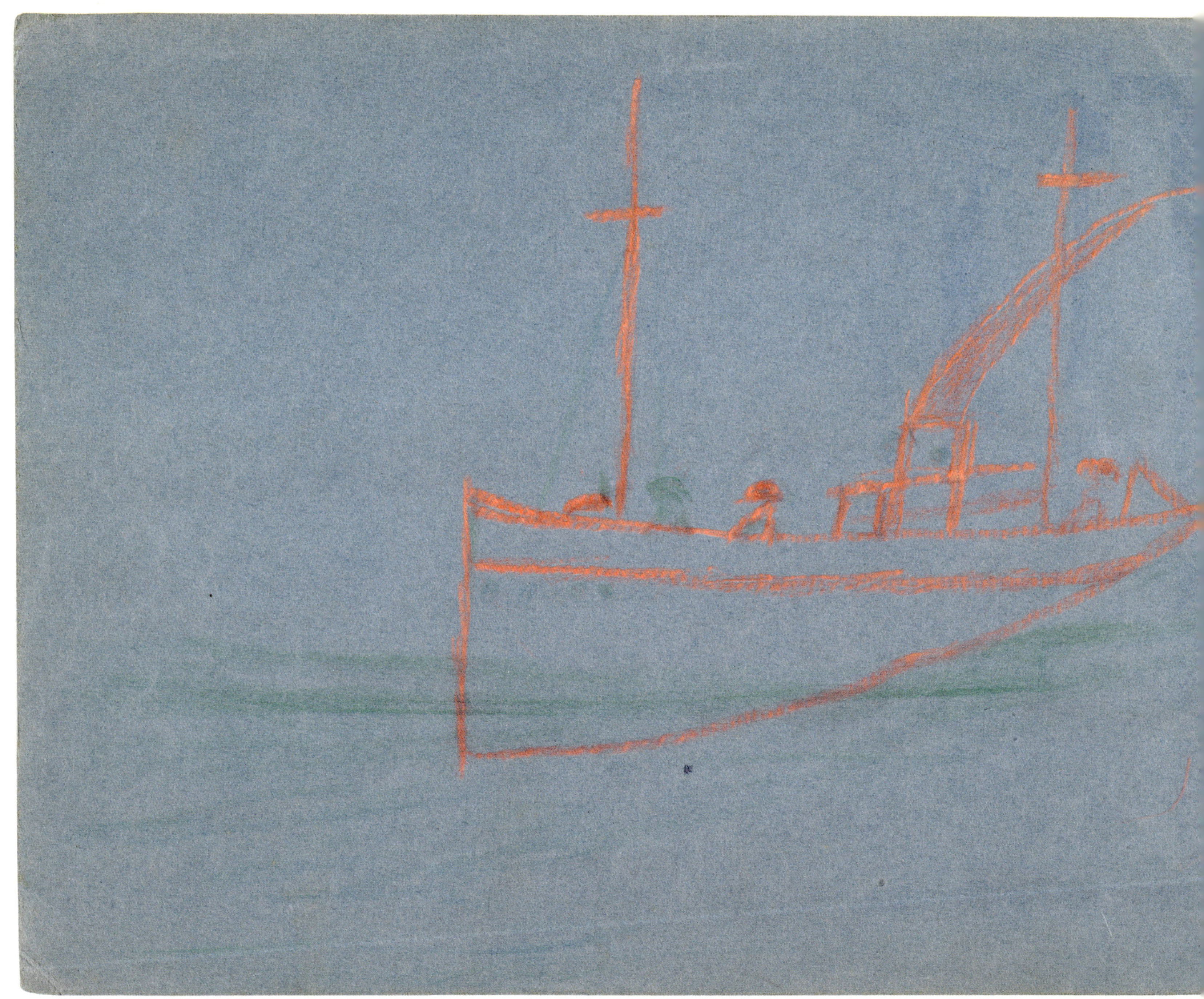

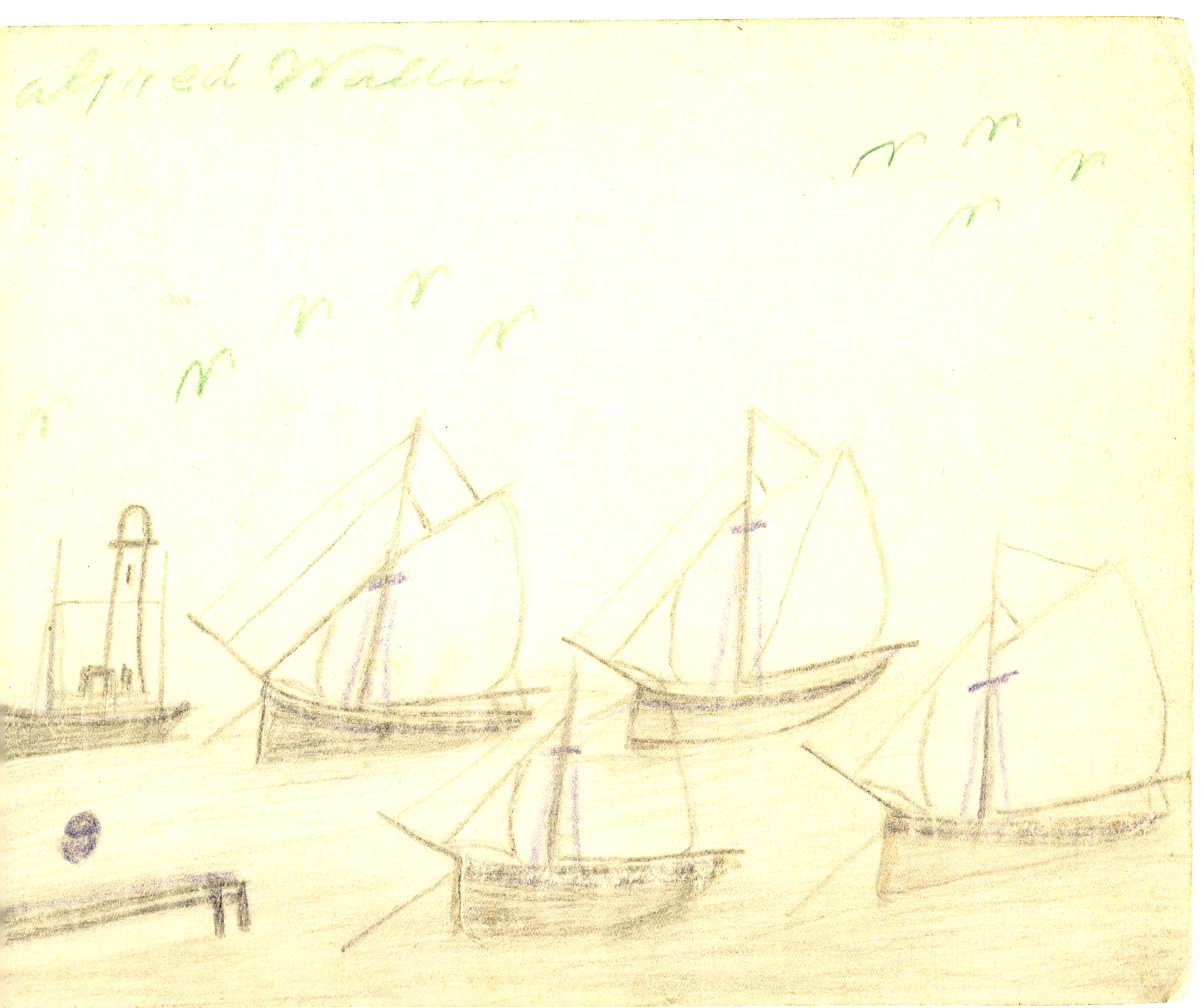

alfred wallis

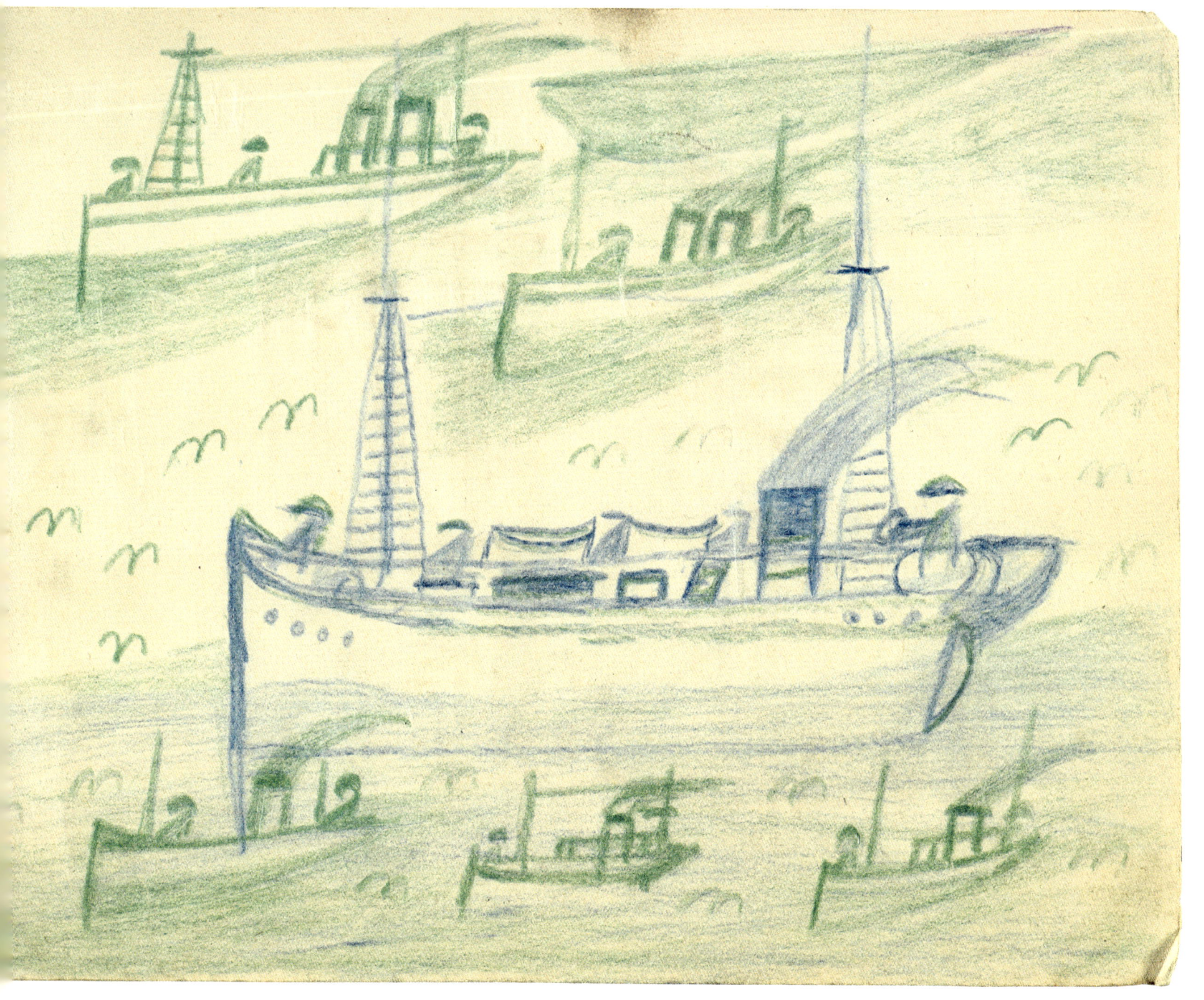

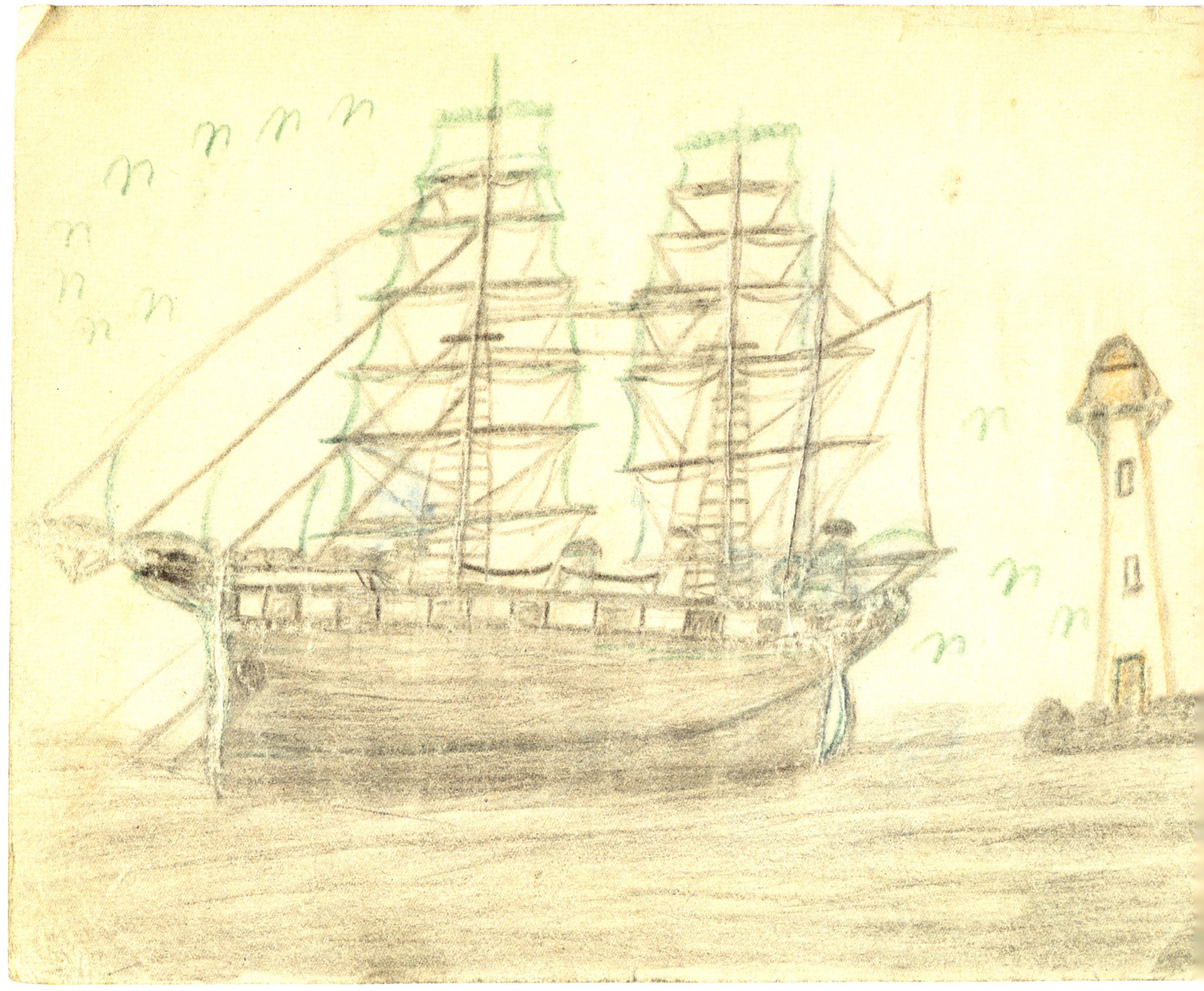

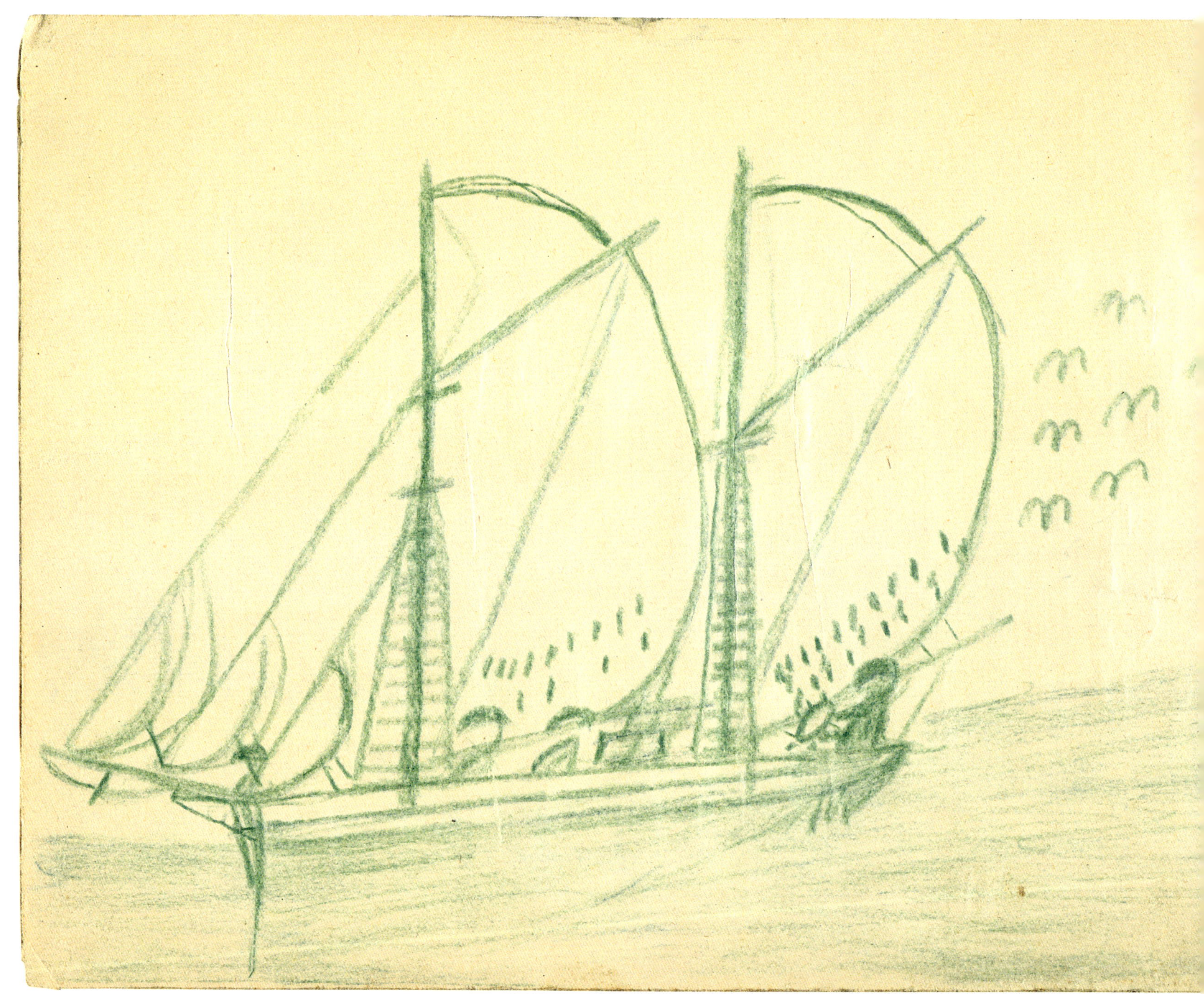

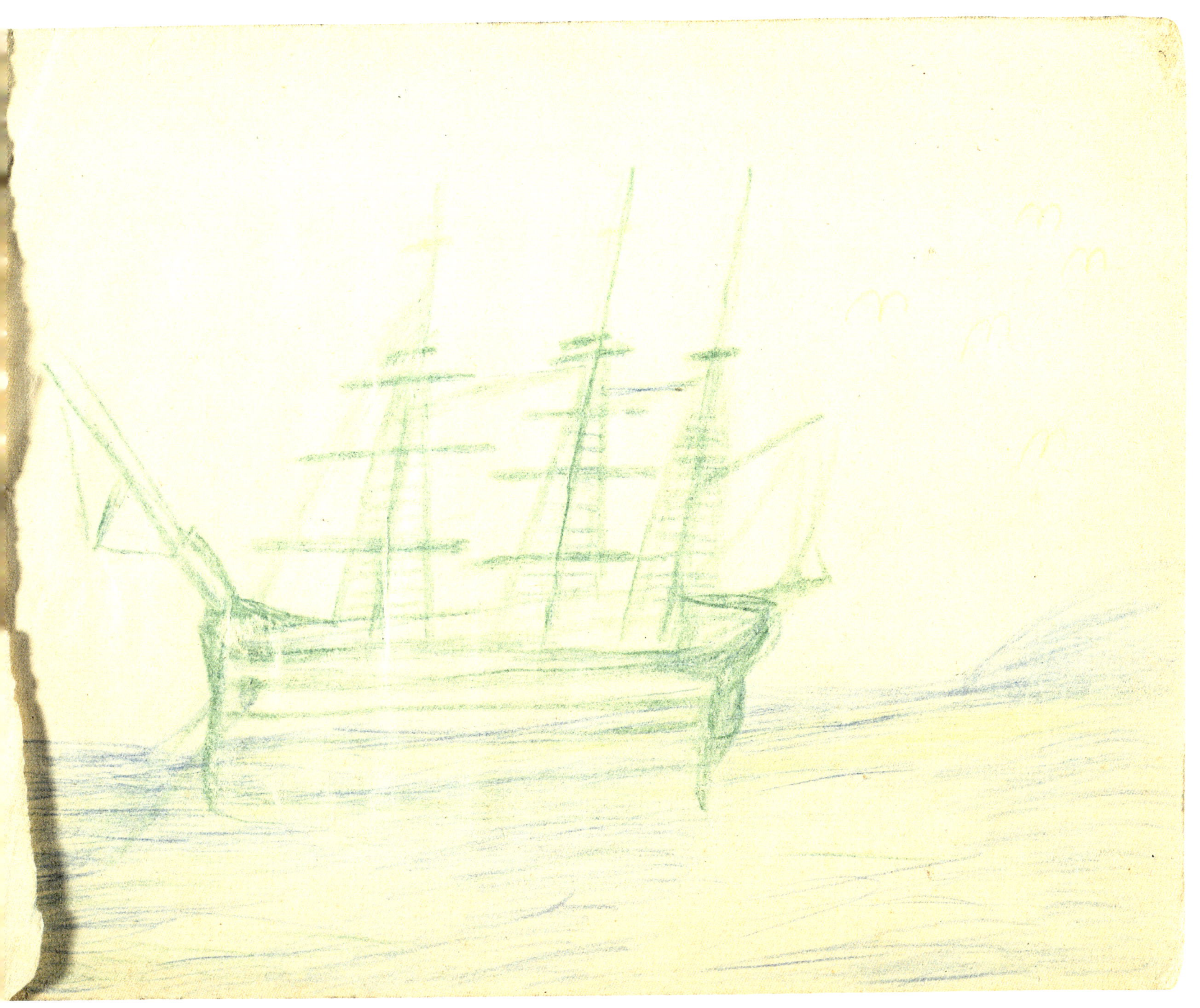

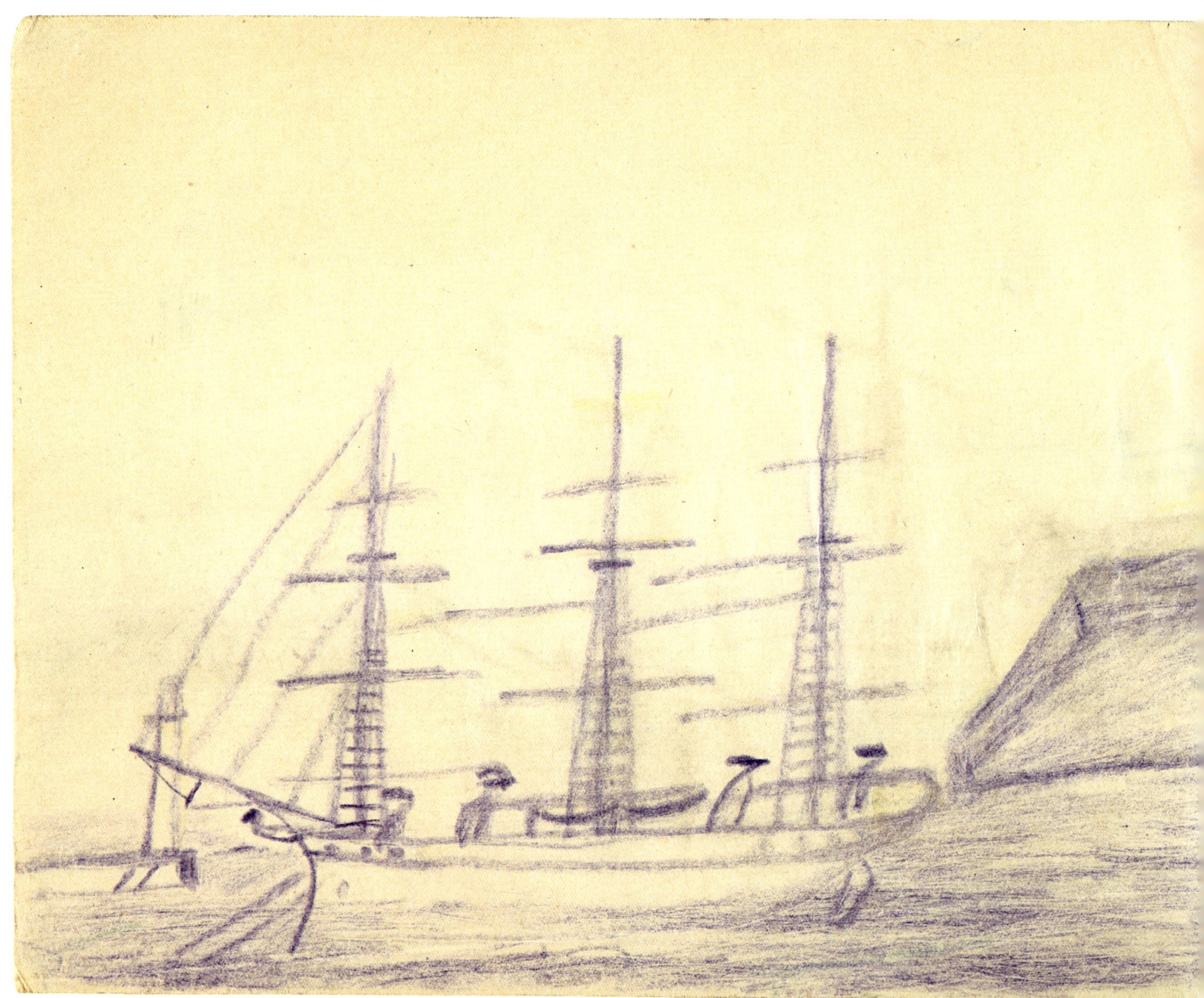

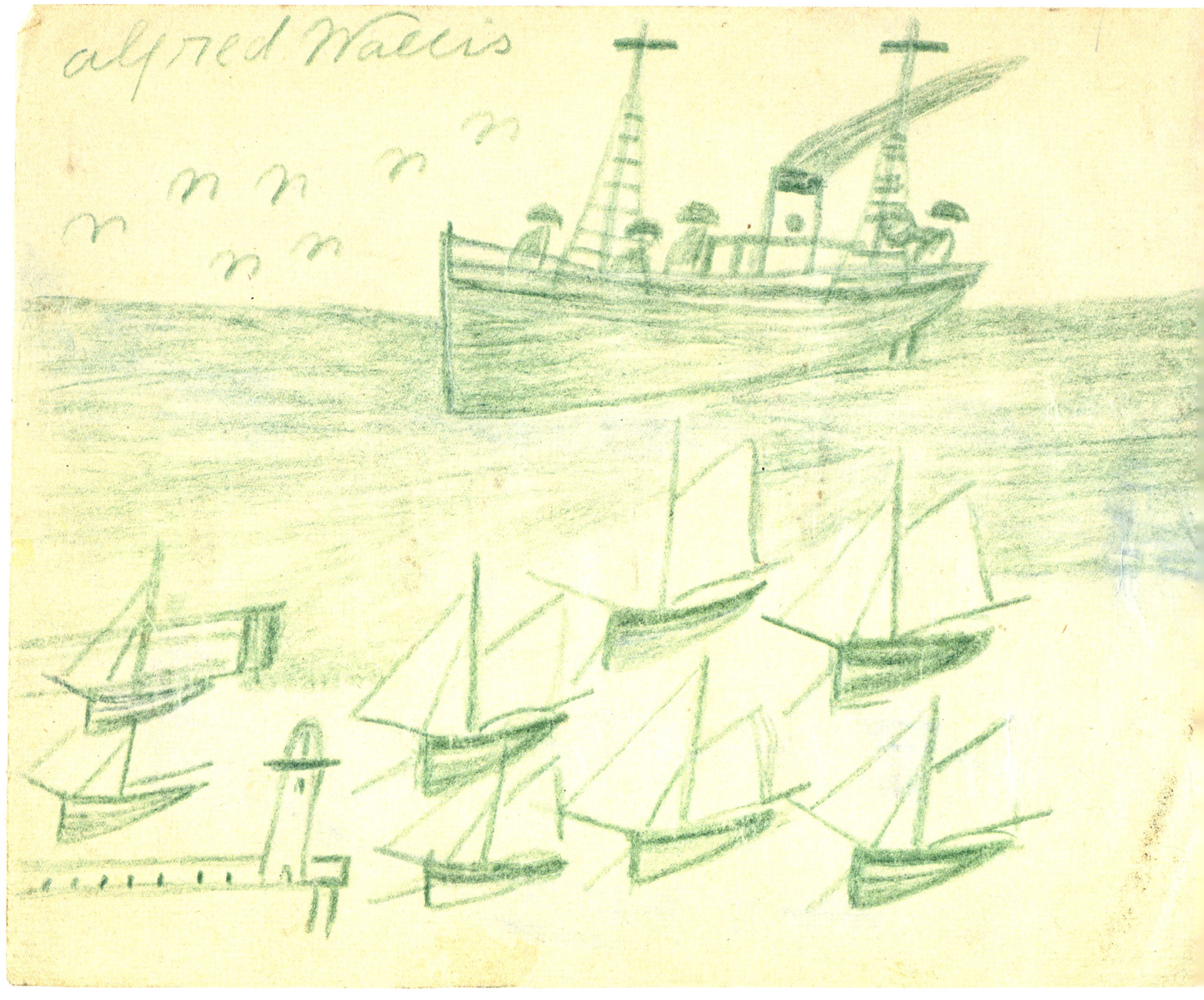
alfred Wallis

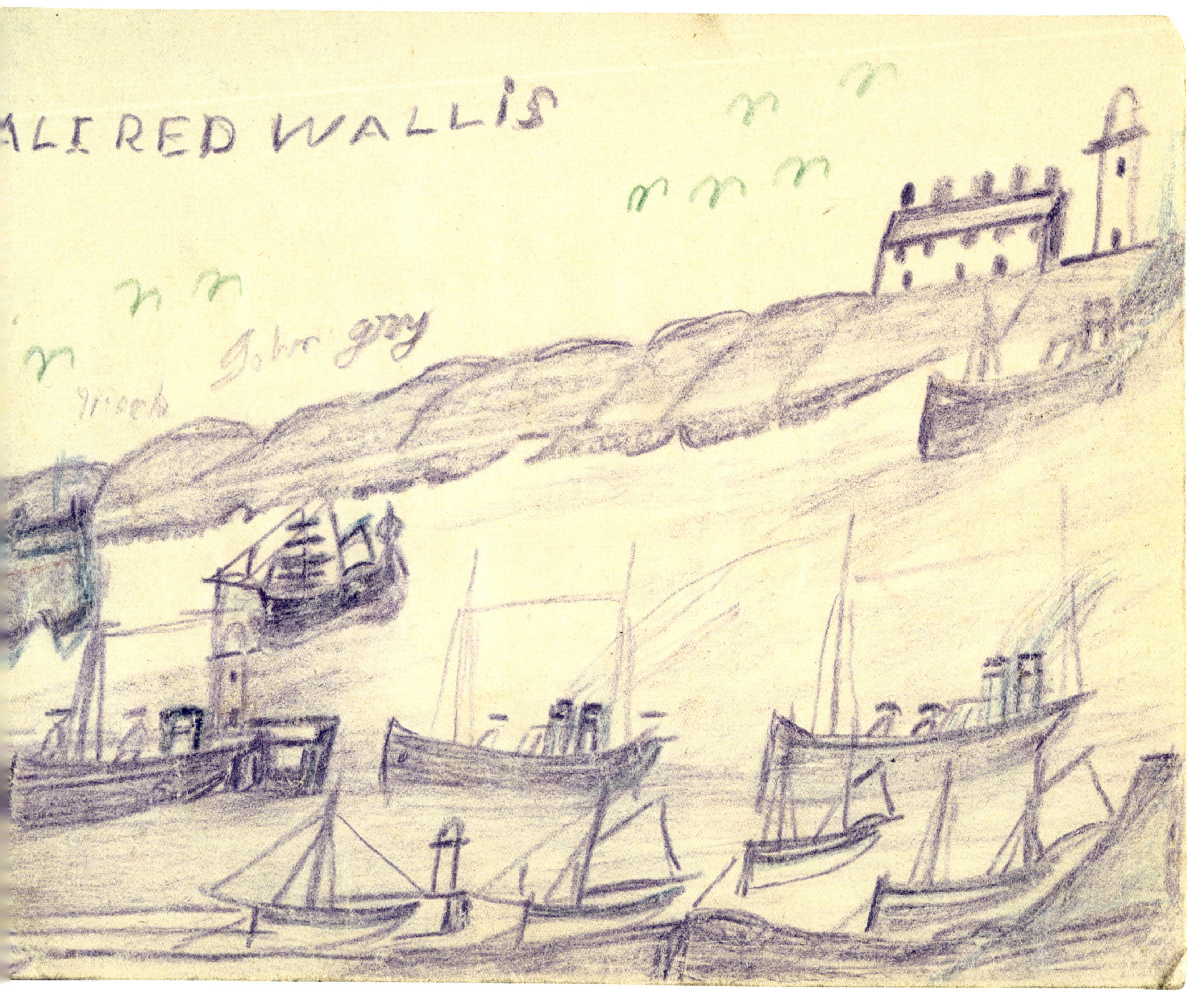
ALFRED WALLIS
John gray
pinah

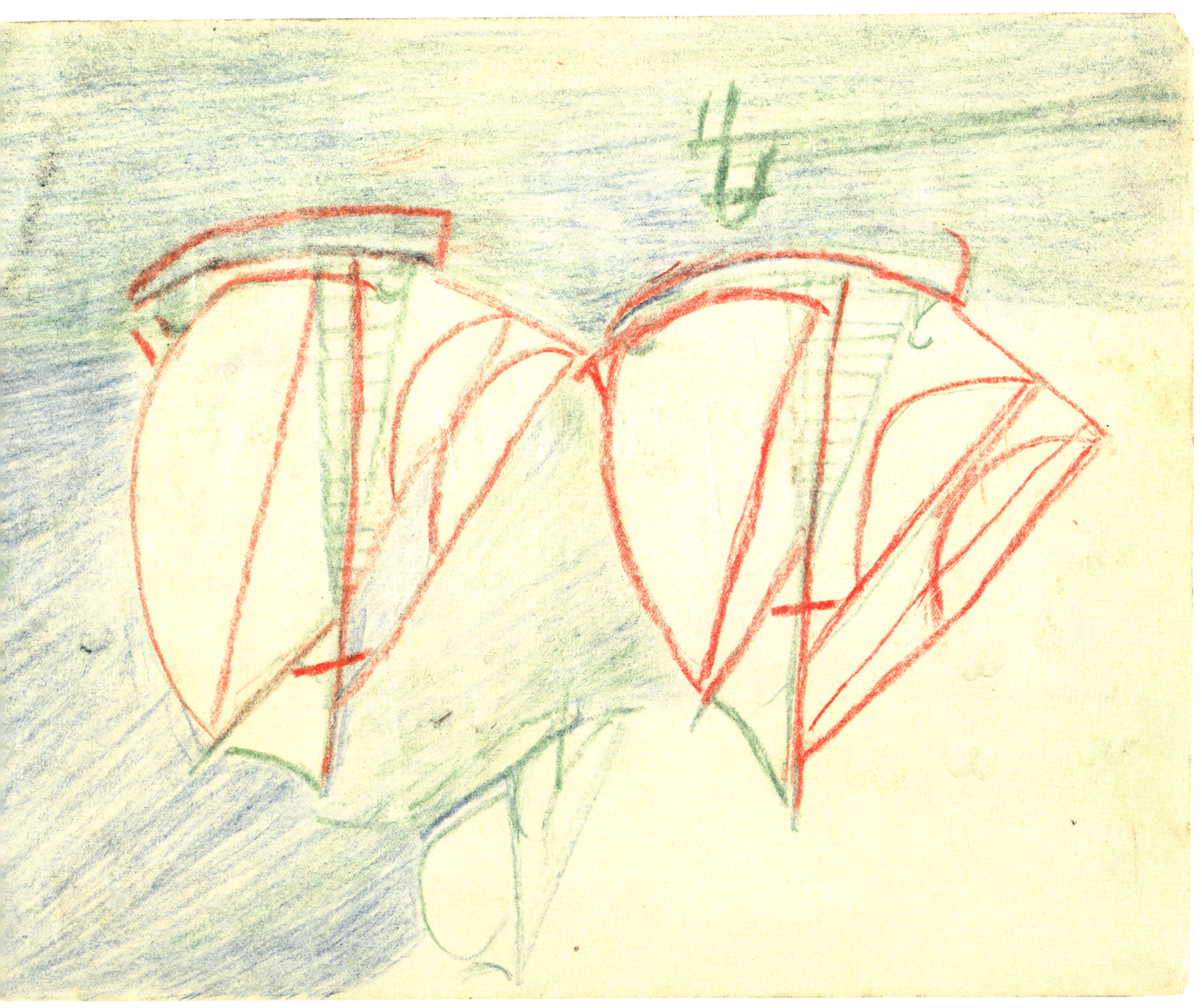

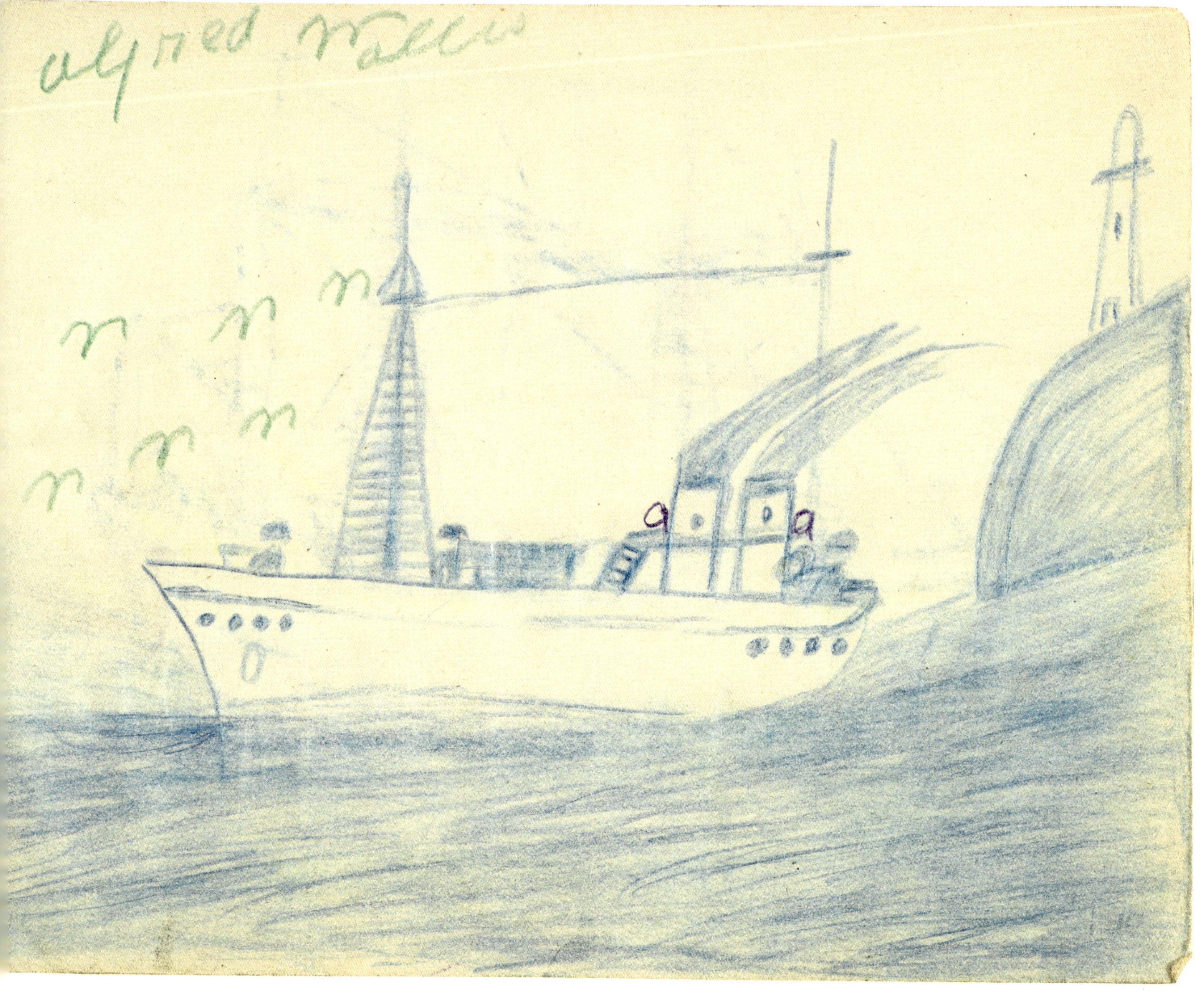
alfred wallis

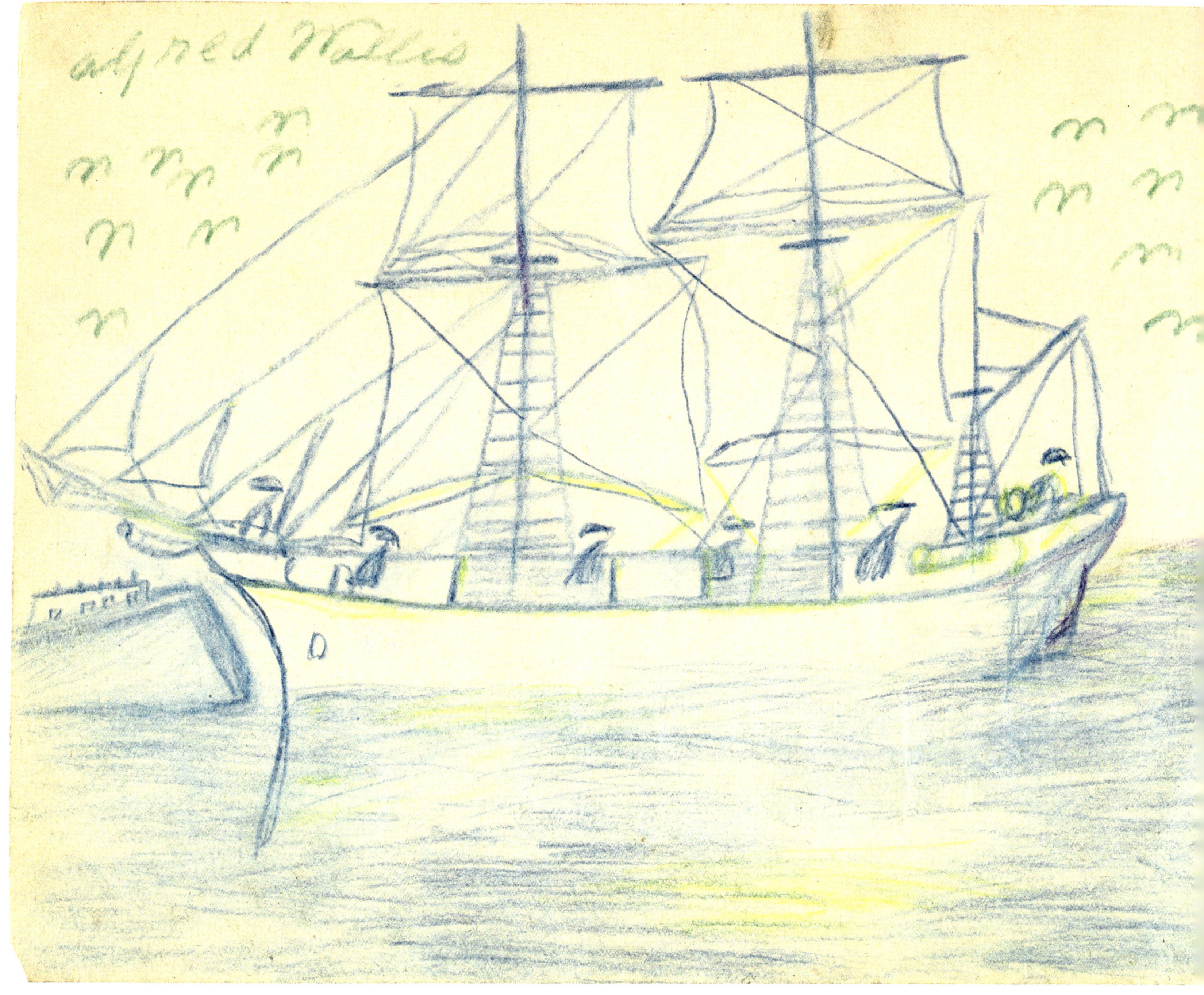

75

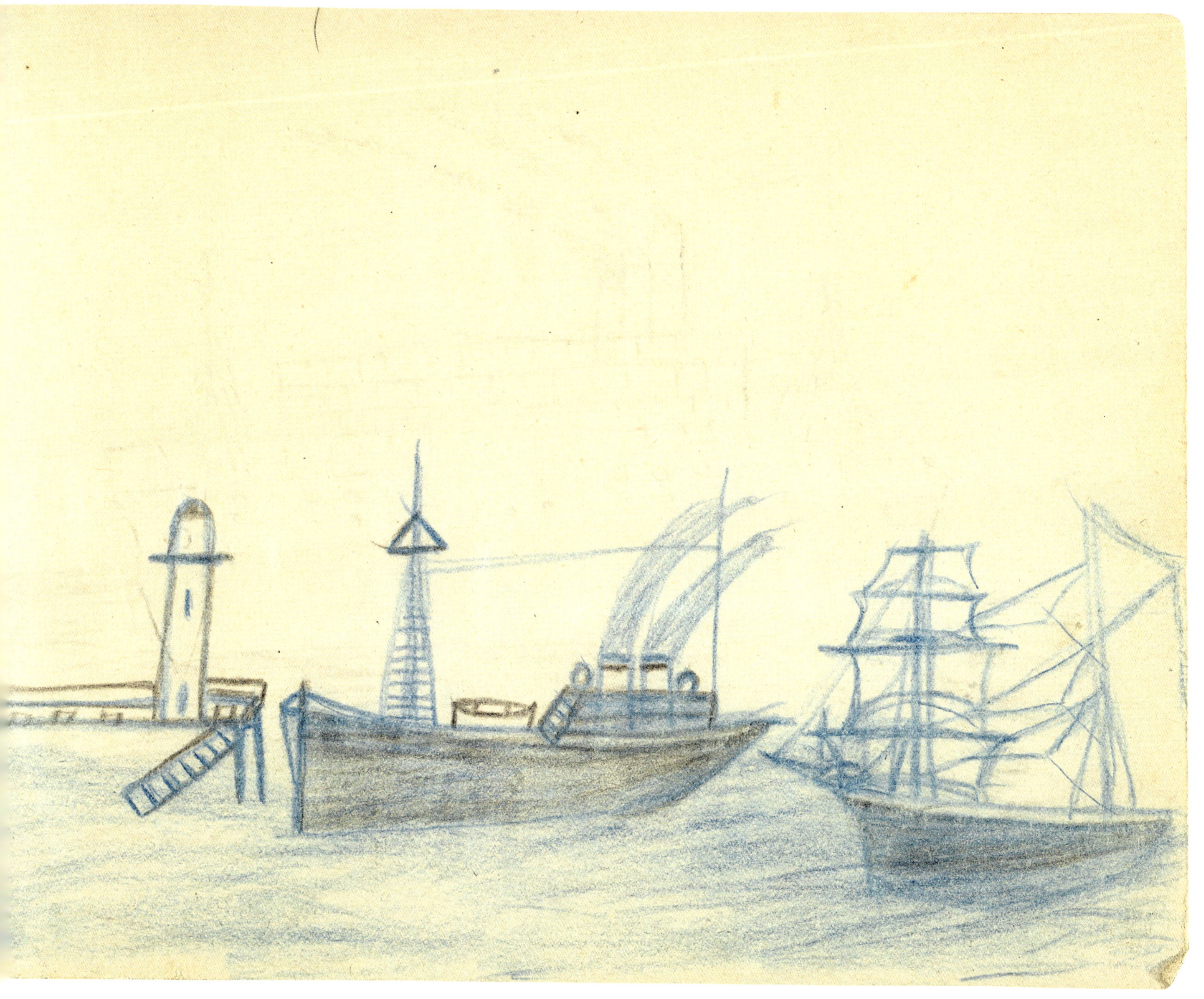

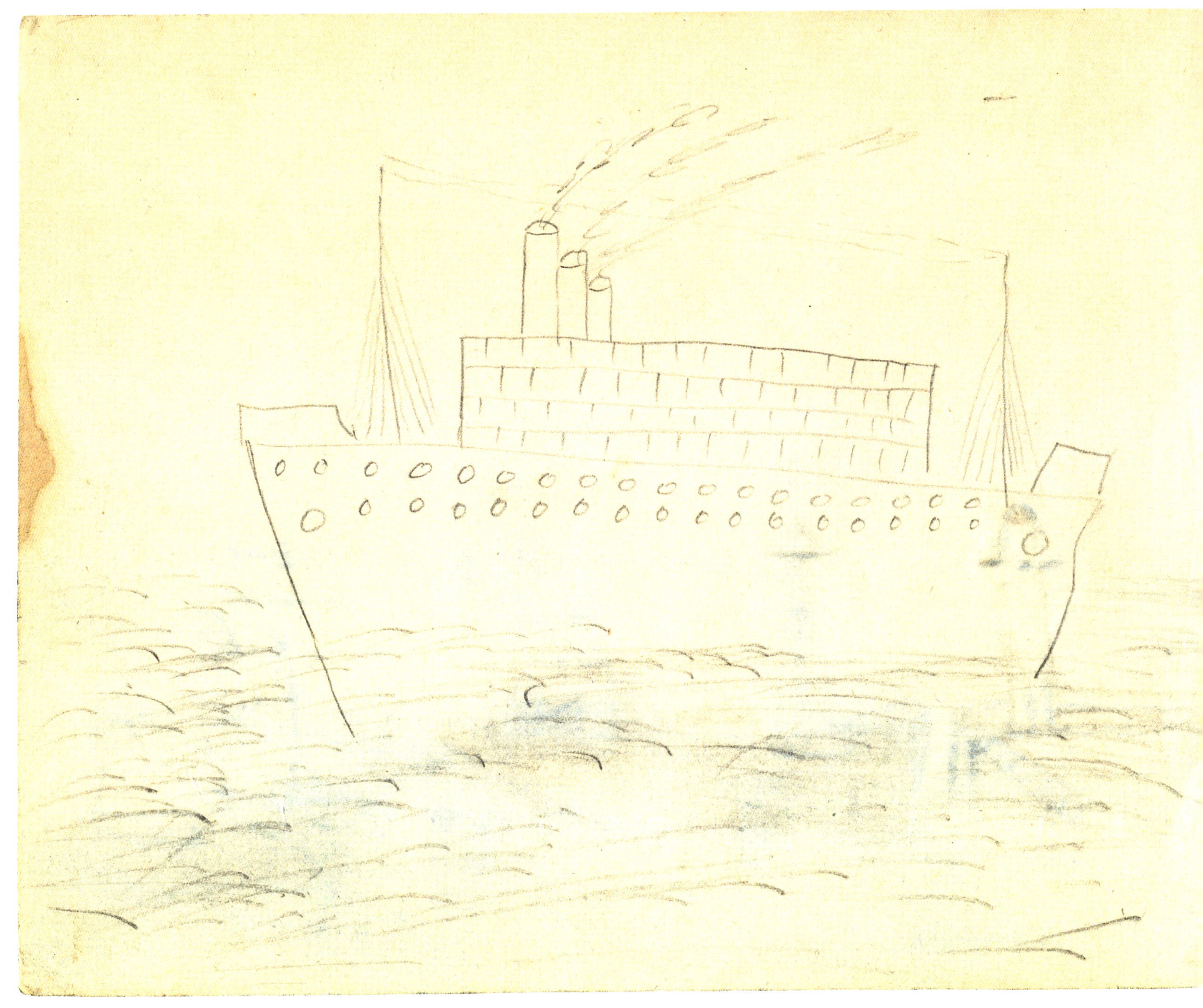

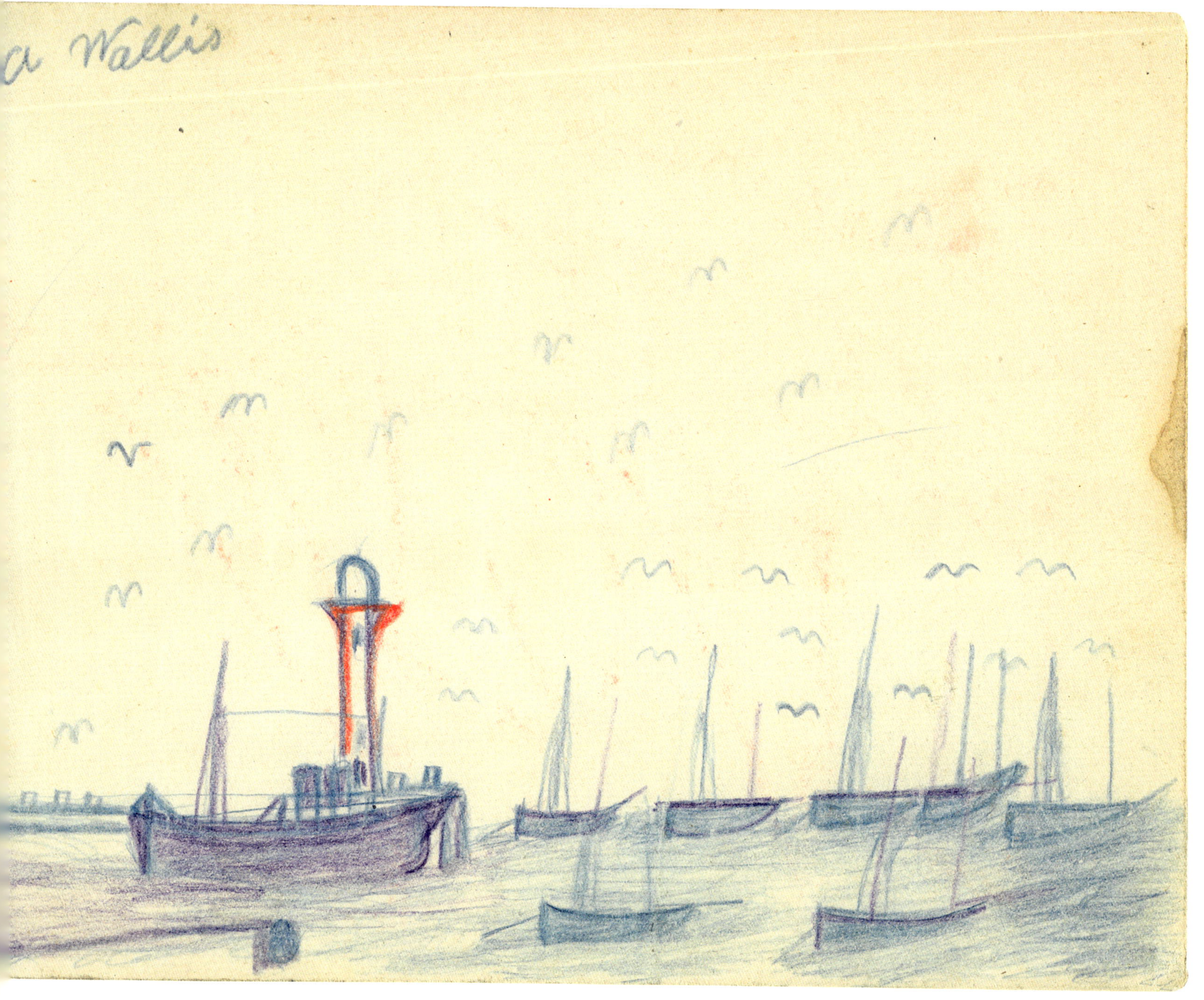
a Wallis

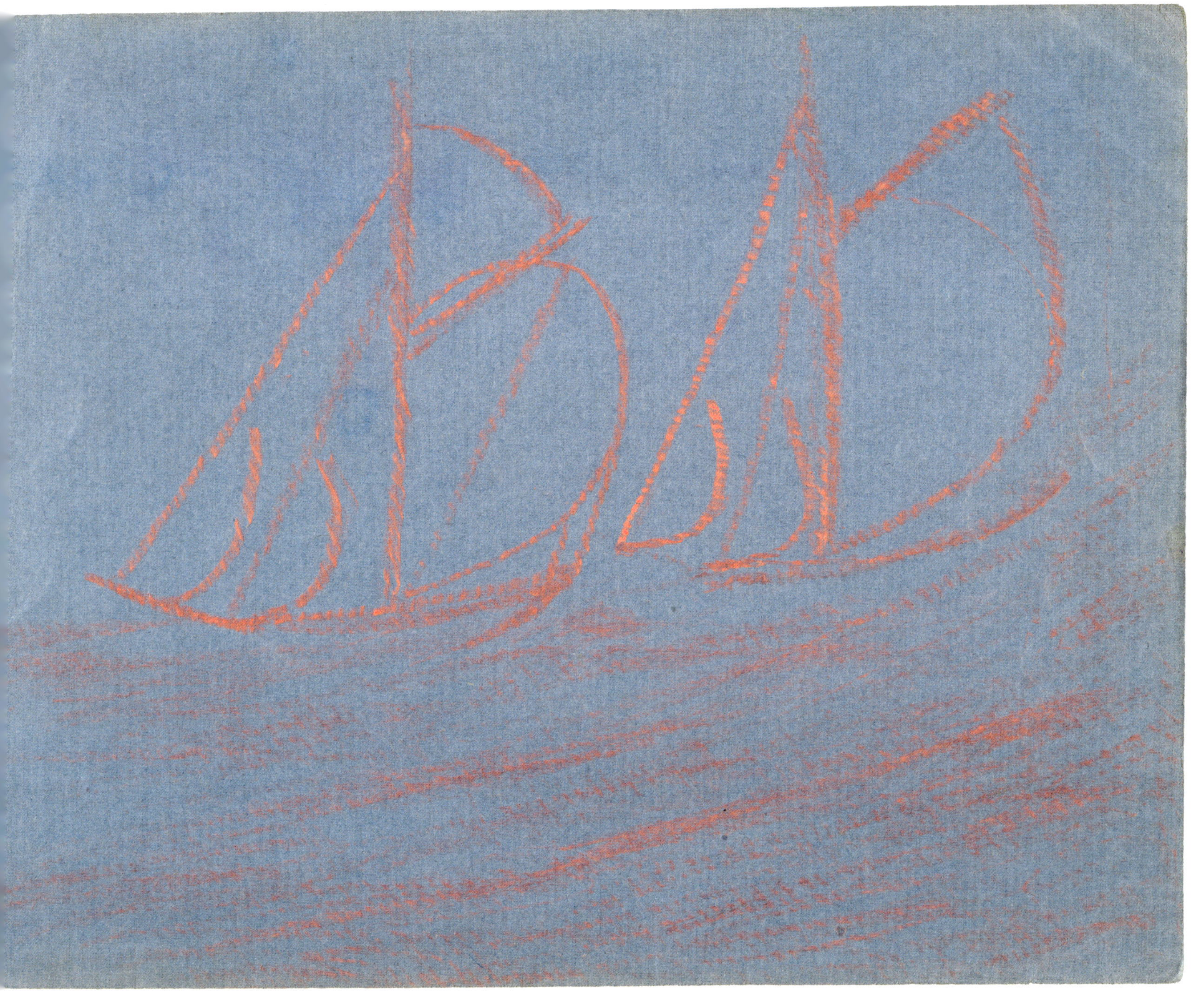

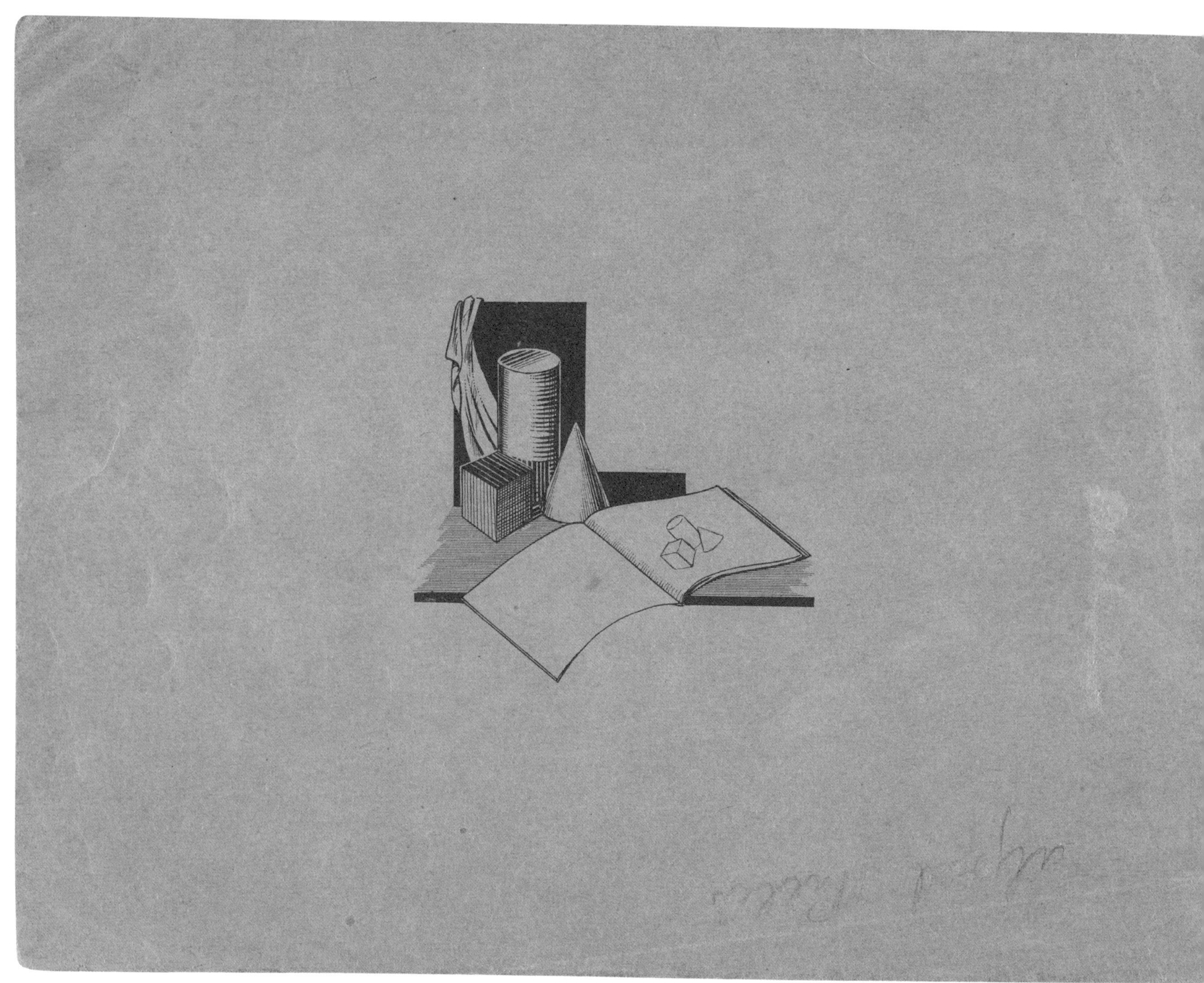